MW01717148

A DICTIONARY OF LITERARY, DRAMATIC, AND CINEMATIC TERMS

Second Edition

SYLVAN BARNET *Tufts University*
MORTON BERMAN *Boston University*
WILLIAM BURTO *Lowell State College*

LITTLE, BROWN AND COMPANY *Boston*

COPYRIGHT © 1960, 1971 BY LITTLE, BROWN AND COMPANY (INC.)

ALL RIGHTS RESERVED. NO PART OF THIS BOOK MAY BE REPRODUCED IN ANY FORM OR BY ANY ELECTRONIC OR MECHANICAL MEANS INCLUDING INFORMATION STORAGE AND RETRIEVAL SYSTEMS WITHOUT PERMISSION IN WRITING FROM THE PUBLISHER, EXCEPT BY A REVIEWER WHO MAY QUOTE BRIEF PASSAGES IN A REVIEW.

LIBRARY OF CONGRESS CATALOG CARD NO. 74-145572

ISBN 0-316-08194-9

16 15 14 13 12

SEM

Printed simultaneously in Canada by
Little, Brown & Company (Canada) Limited

PRINTED IN THE UNITED STATES OF AMERICA

The first edition of this book was entitled *A Dictionary of Literary Terms.*

PREFACE

When Boswell asked Dr. Johnson "What is Poetry?" Johnson gave the inevitable reply: "Why, Sir, it is much easier to say what it is not. We all *know* what light is; but it is not easy to tell what it is." It is not even easy to tell what a literary term is in its most mechanical aspect. The sort of definition that Dickens's Bitzer gave of a horse cannot so easily be given of a literary term:

> "Bitzer," said Thomas Gradgrind. "Your definition of a horse."
>
> "Quadruped. Graminivorous. Forty teeth, namely twenty-four grinders, four eye-teeth, and twelve incisive. Sheds coat in the spring; in marshy countries sheds hoofs, too. Hoofs hard, but requiring to be shod with iron. Age known by marks in mouth." Thus (and much more) Bitzer.
>
> "Now girl number twenty," said Mr. Gradgrind. "You know what a horse is."

The following definitions, one hopes, have more life in them than Bitzer's horse, but they are only rough approximations of the ways in which some critics use the terms defined. These terms ought not to tyrannize the reader; rather, they may in part be the means whereby he takes (in Henry James's word) "possession" of literature.

Words defined are in **bold face.** A word in a definition preceded by the symbol ° is itself defined in its proper alphabetical position.

S. B.
M. B.
W. B.

abstract. See °concrete.

Absurd, Theater of the. Drama of such writers as Eugène Ionesco and Samuel Beckett in France and Harold Pinter in England that imitates the absurdity of man's existence. "Everything, as I see it, is an abberration," Ionesco has said. Though the plays are serious, they may contain extravagantly comic scenes in depicting a reality that is absurd, illogical, senseless, a world of futility and meaningless clichés. In Ionesco's *The Chairs* (1952) an elderly couple rush about, filling a room with chairs for nonexistent visitors. Old age is a fact, but an absurdity, too, and old people are incomprehensible. At the end of *The Chairs,* an orator, who is to deliver a solemn talk about the truths of life, turns out to be deaf and dumb and merely makes unintelligible noises and gestures to the invisible crowd. Ionesco summarizes the theme of *The Chairs* (*New York Times,* June 1, 1958): "I have tried to deal . . . with emptiness, with frustration, with this world, at once fleeting and crushing. The characters I have used are not fully conscious of their spiritual rootlessness, but they feel it instinctively and emotionally." One basis of man's inability to communicate, and one which the "Absurd" dramatists seize upon, is the corruption of language. The absurdity of trying to communicate by means of a debased language is dramatized by Ionesco in *The Bald Soprano* (1950), where the characters speak in clichés. Because the characters are incomprehensible and the happenings illogical and baffling, the spectators cannot simply sit back in ease, but are continually challenged to grasp the play's meaning. (Consult M. Esslin, *The Theatre of the Absurd.*)

accent. See °versification.

acrostic. A poem in which certain letters in successive lines (normally the initial letter of each line) form a word when read down. Here is a tribute to Dryden.

> D eep rolls on deep in thy majestic line.
> R ich music and the stateliest march combine;
> Y et, who that hears its high harmonious strain
> D eems not thy genius thou didst half profane?
> E xhausting thy great power of song on themes
> N ot worthy of its strong, effulgent beams.

(Consult C. C. Bombaugh, *Oddities and Curiosities,* pp. 39–49, 332–35.)

act. A main division in drama or opera. Act divisions probably arose in Rome and derive ultimately from the Greek practice of separating episodes in a play by choral interludes, but Greek (and probably Roman) plays were performed without interruption, for the choral interludes were part of the plays themselves. The division of °Elizabethan plays into five acts, often the work of editors rather than of authors, is usually of small significance. Frequently an act division today (commonly indicated by lowering the curtain and turning up the house-lights) denotes change in locale and lapse of time. A **scene** is a smaller unit, either: (1) a division with no change of locale or abrupt shift of time; or (2) a division consisting of an actor or group of actors on the stage (according to the second definition, the departure or entrance of an actor changes the composition of the group and thus introduces a new scene). In an entirely different sense, the scene is the locale where a work is set. (See also °plot.)

action. See °plot.

aesthetic distance. See °psychical distance.

Aesthetic Movement. Fairly early in the nineteenth century there developed in France a devotion to beauty not because beauty reflected a Divine Mind, but because it was a good in itself in a materialistic world which otherwise seemed chaotic and depressing. The Aesthetic Movement thus rejected theories which held that the value of literature is somehow related to morality or to some sort of usefulness, and instead advocated, in defiance of much tradition and of the bourgeoisie, the independence of art from any moral or °didactic end. The implications of its slogan, "*l'art pour l'art*" (**art for art's sake**), are entertainingly presented by Théophile Gautier, in the preface to his *Mademoiselle de Maupin*. But of his attack on the idea that art should be useful ("The most useful place in any house," he argues, "is the water closet"), one can perhaps ask, with Samuel Butler, "What is art, that it should have a sake?" In England (during the last decades of the century, when it flourished in opposition to Victorian moral earnestness) the movement is chiefly associated with Walter Pater and Oscar Wilde, though there is a gap between Pater's ascetic desire "to burn with a hard, gem-like flame" and Wilde's somewhat flippant desire to live up to his blue china. Behind the aesthetes' concern with sensation is a tradition that goes back to Keats, Tennyson, and Rossetti, but in aesthetic writing the quest for sensation commonly suggests weariness or spiritual collapse. The term ***fin de siècle*** ("end of century"), which earlier had occasionally connoted progress, came, because of this movement, to imply **decadence** – a falling off, marked by a sense of ennui and/or frustration, a languid concern for mere polish and a freakish interest in the unusual. (If capitalized, **Decadence** frequently refers to the Aesthetic Movement.) When in Wilde's *The Picture of Dorian Gray* a woman says, "Nowadays all the married men live like bachelors and all the bachelors like married men," the weary explanation is "*Fin de siècle.*" (Consult H. Jackson, *The Eighteen Nineties*; W. Gaunt, *The Aesthetic Adventure*; and R. L. Peters, "Toward an 'Un-Definition' of Decadent," *Journal of Aesthetics and Art Criticism*, 18 [1959], 258–64.)

agon. A debate in a Greek play, normally between the chief actor (the protagonist) and his antagonist. (See also, under °comedy, the remarks on Old Comedy.)

Alexandrine. See °versification.

allegory. When St. Augustine noted that we derive pleasure from thinking of holy men as sheep, he was commenting on the pleasure afforded by allegory. Frequently an allegory is a narrative wherein abstractions (such as virtue, fear, love) are made concrete (Mr. Virtue, etc.), for the purpose of effectively communicating a moral. The characters and their actions interest us, and we absorb the moral ideas they embody. Thus, in Bunyan's *The Pilgrim's Progress*, a man named Christian journeys to the Celestial City, encountering on his way Mr. Worldly Wiseman, the Giant Despair, and others. Dorothy Sayers, in the introduction to her translation of Dante's *Divine Comedy: Hell*, says that John Doe's desire to do something or other, and his simultaneous fear of the consequences, can be allegorized by having a knight, Desire, attack a castle guarded by Fear. Desire is battered severely, but is roused by his squire Shame, is healed by a lady, Hope, and so forth. But allegory is not confined to the invention of concrete fictions. Dante, for example, used Biblical and historical characters, seeing them as embodiments of a further significance or higher truth. Moreover, allegory can make use of landscape as well as people, giving a significance to mountains, valleys, roads, etc. Some critics insist that an allegory is thus a narrative wherein a moral significance stands behind the visible presentation, or a narrative with a continuous system of equivalents. But narrative is not essential, nor are abstractions; allegory is simply the presentation of something by something else. (See also °symbolism. Consult C. S. Lewis, *The Allegory of Love*; A. Fletcher, *Allegory*.)

A **parable** is a short narrative from which a moral can be drawn, such as Christ's tale of the Good Samaritan (Luke 10:30–7). It may (but need not) be an allegory, wherein, say, each character stands for an abstraction that otherwise would be hard to grasp. Commonly the parable lacks the *detailed* correspondence of an allegory. For example, in the parable of the wise and foolish virgins (Matthew 25:1–13), the oil does not stand for anything.

alliteration. See °versification.

allusion. A reference to something, real or fictitious, outside of the work. Thus, in T. S. Eliot's "The Love Song of J. Alfred Prufrock," the speaker says, "I am not Prince Hamlet." If an allusion is obscure, it may be wasted, but an allusion that is recognized (such as Eliot's) can effectively call up relevant associations.

ambiguity. See °figurative language.

amphibrach and **amphimacer.** See °figurative language.

anachronism. Something out of its proper time. The clock that strikes in Shakespeare's *Julius Caesar* is an anachronism, for there were no striking clocks in Caesar's Rome. Although we are often distressed or amused by anachronisms in literature, earlier ages felt differently. Chaucer, for example, turns his ancient Greeks and Trojans into medieval knights, holding that men do not change much over the ages; and medieval artists painted the Holy Family in medieval garb. (For the idea that anachronisms may be deliberately used to make the past seem contemporary, see S. L. Bethell, *Shakespeare and the Popular Dramatic Tradition*, Ch. 4.)

Anacreontic poetry. Named for Anacreon (Greek poet of the sixth century B.C.), who sang of wine and women. Among his imitators in England were Robert Herrick and Tom Moore, who wrote graceful °lyrics of Cupid and Bacchus.

anacrusis. See °versification.

***anagnorisis*.** See °tragedy and °plot.

anagram. A rearrangement of the letters of a word to spell another word, especially a relevant one. Example: astronomer = moonstarer. Lewis Carroll found "Wild agitator! Means well" in the name of Prime Minister William Ewart Gladstone. (Consult C. C. Bombaugh, *Oddities and Curiosities*, pp. 49–57, 335–59.)

analogue. Something comparable in certain respects to something else; specifically, in literature, a tale or aspect of a tale resembling another, though no direct relationship can be traced. Material (*e.g.*, °plot or °style) from which later material is derived is not an analogue but the **source.**

analysis. See °criticism.

anapest (adjective: **anapestic**). See °versification.

anaphora. Repetition of a word or phrase at the beginning of successive lines of poetry or successive clauses of prose. Example, from *Othello:*

> Farewell the tranquil mind. Farewell content!
> Farewell the plumèd troop, and the big wars.

anatomy. See °satire.

anecdote. Originally, unpublished facts of history; now, a short account of an °episode, usually of biographical interest. Unlike most good short stories, anecdotes depend less on artistic arrangement than on an inherently entertaining episode.

angle. See °shot.

antagonist. See °plot.

anticlimax. A sudden drop, sometimes deliberately comic (as in Aldous Huxley's conclusion to a love poem: "And there we sit in blissful calm, / Quietly sweating palm to palm"), sometimes merely inept. If the work of art peters out after a °climax (see °plot), the weak ending is anticlimactic. But notice that great art often ends quietly. °Tragedies, for example, do not usually end with a death, but with some comment on the death, and this comment is not anticlimactic unless it competes with the climax and fails. (See also °bathos, under °pathos).

antimasque. See °drama.

antistrophe. See °ode.

antithesis. See °form.

aphorism (or ***sententia;*** plural: ***sententiae***). A pointed statement alleging a truth, such as Pope's "Hope springs eternal in the human breast," or Aristotle's "Education is learning to take pleasure in the right things." If the aphorism has become common property with a fixed form (*e.g.*, "A rolling stone gathers no moss"), it is a **proverb.** A proverb usually offers a concrete instance with a generalization lurking in it, *e.g.*, "A stitch in time saves nine." In imaginative literature of the Renaissance and later, more often than not the proverb is used with an °ironic or comic effect, the speaker (*e.g.*, Polonius) demonstrating his inability to deal with the complexities of his situation. If an aphorism gives advice on behavior (*e.g.*, Bacon's "Some books are to be tasted, others to be swallowed, and some few to be chewed and digested"), it is sometimes called a **maxim. Gnomic poetry** consists of aphorisms, proverbs, and maxims. Primitive poets are often gnomic, but so, too, are sophisticated poets. Robert Frost especially catches a gnomic mood:

> Why abandon a belief
> Merely because it ceases to be true.
> Cling to it long enough, and not a doubt
> It will turn true again, for so it goes.

By virtue of their conciseness, aphorisms often have a worldly-wise or satiric tone, as in Swift's "Every man desires to live long; but no man would be old." (Consult M. Hodgart, *Satire*, pp. 150–58; and W. H. Auden and L. Kronenberger, *The Viking Book of Aphorisms.*)

apocrypha. See °canon.

Apollonian and **Dionysian.** Friedrich Nietzsche suggested, in *The Birth of Tragedy* (1872), that Greek °tragedy, usually considered calm and poised, was not the product of such quiet minds as was usually thought. If tragedy showed light and beauty (over which Apollo presided), it was nevertheless also indebted to Dionysus, god of the vine and hence of wine, who represented the savage, frenzied, ecstatic, irrational, buried self-assertions of the mind. That is, Greek tragedy was the product of a tension between the Dionysian violent self-assertion or ecstatic union and the Apollonian sense of moderation and of detached rational contemplation of the external order. Apollonian is often associated with °classicism, and Dionysian with °romanticism (see under °classic).

apology. A defense (not necessarily contrite). Examples are Sir Philip Sidney's *Apology for Poetry,* Cardinal Newman's *Apologia pro vita sua.*

apostrophe. See °figurative language.

Arcadia. See °Golden Age and °pastoral.

archaism. See °diction.

archetype. The common meaning, "the original pattern or model from which all other things of the same kind are made," is somewhat broader than its meaning in literary criticism. Carl G. Jung, the Swiss psychologist, in *Contributions to Analytical Psychology,* postulates the existence of a "collective unconscious" in men's minds, an inheritance in the brain consisting of "countless typical experiences [such as birth, escape from danger, selection of a mate] of our ancestors." These experiences, such as perception of the perpetual rising and setting (birth and death, one might say) of the sun, manifest themselves in dreams, °myths, and °literature (see °motif). In *The Rime of the Ancient Mariner,* for example, Coleridge treats the traditional (archetypal, some would say) theme of death and rebirth: the ship suffers a deathlike calm and then is miraculously restored to motion. Among the archetypes are the Hero (savior, deliverer), the Terrible Mother (witch, cruel stepmother – even the wolf "grandmother" in the tale of Little Red Ridinghood), and the Wise Old Man (magician). Because (the theory holds) both writer and reader share unconscious memories, the tale an author tells, derived from the collective unconscious, may strangely move the reader, stirring his collective unconscious. As Maud Bodkin, in *Archetypal Patterns in Poetry,* puts it, there is something within us that "leaps in response to the effective presentation in poetry of an ancient theme." (Consult N. Frye, "My Credo," *The Kenyon Review,* 13 [1951], 92–110; N. Frye, *Anatomy of Criticism;* and L. Lane, "The Literary Archetype: Some Reconsiderations," *Journal of Aesthetics and Art Criticism,* 13 [1954], 226–32.)

art for art's sake. See °Aesthetic Movement.

aside. See °convention and °soliloquy.

assonance. See °versification.

atmosphere. The air (calm, sinister, oppressive, etc.) breathed by the reader as he enters into the world of a literary work. It might also be called **mood,** but ought not to be confused with °tone. An atmosphere of childlike simplicity or of mystery may be set up, partly by the objects described and partly by the °style of the description. The **setting,** or locale (which can include time – such as a hospital in Milan during World War I) often contributes to atmosphere.

Attic sentence. See °style.

aubade. A morning serenade, or a °lyric concerned with the dawn, such as "Hark, hark, the lark at heaven's gate sings," in Shakespeare's *Cymbeline,* II.iii.22–30.

aube. A °lyric sung by one of the partners in a courtly love affair, regretting that the coming of dawn will part the lovers. (Consult R. E. Kaske, in *Chaucer Criticism,* II, ed. R. J. Schoeck and J. Taylor.)

Augustan Age. Named for the reign of Augustus (27 B.C.–14 A.D.), when Roman literature was at its height, with Ovid, Horace, Catullus, and Vergil. Because English authors of the first third of the eighteenth century admired these Romans, and because it was sometimes felt by both those Englishmen and later scholars that the two periods had a common concern for gentlemanliness and urbanity, the term "Augustan Age" is applied to both periods. In England, Addison, Steele, Swift, and Pope are the notable Augustans. (See °Enlightenment, and °classic.) In France the reign of Louis XIV has sometimes been characterized as Augustan. (Consult P. Fussell, *The Rhetorical World of Augustan Humanism.*)

auteur theory. See °director.

autobiography. See °biography.

ballad. The **traditional** or **popular ballad** is a story told in a song which has been passed down by word of mouth from singer to singer. Ballads were common in the fifteenth century, and one ("Judas") is known to have come down from the thirteenth century. Whatever their original authorship, they became the property of the common people, who sang them, polished them by conscious or unconscious alterations, and taught them to their children. This **oral transmission** of traditional material probably shows itself in the impersonal tone (the singer rarely sings about his attitude toward the story) and in the highly effective abrupt transitions in the terse narrative. Weak verses have probably been expelled or forgotten, and the result is often a series of effectively juxtaposed pictures. Perhaps, too, oral transmission accounts for some of the nonsense lines frequently found in the **refrain** (repeated lines, or chorus); the nonsense refrain "Every rose is merry in time" is a singer's misunderstanding of "savory, rosemary, thyme." (The student who writes of a "devil-make-hair" attitude similarly illustrates this aspect of the oral tradition.) A common stanza form is a quatrain of alternating lines of iambic tetrameter and iambic trimeter, the trimeter lines rhyming (see °versification). Ballads occasionally employ **incremental repetition,** *i.e.*, the repetition of some previous line or lines, but with a slight variation so as to advance the narrative, as in these lines from "The Cruel Brother":

> "O what will you leave to your father dear?"
> "The silver-shode steed that brought me here."
> "What will you leave to your mother dear?"
> "My velvet pall and my silken gear."

Though the singers are common people, the subjects are frequently noble; the most usual theme is love, often tragic. The simple language and impersonal tone often seem to cover deep feeling, and the refrain often adds either a note of solemn °ritual or a lyrical contrast to the stark tale. Traditional ballads were being produced throughout the nineteenth century, in America commonly by sailors, loggers, and plantation workers (*i.e.*, relatively isolated and illiterate persons), and in rural areas such ballads are still alive. (See °folklore. Consult G. H. Gerould, *The Ballad of Tradition;* M. J. C. Hodgart, *The Ballads;* and *The Viking Book of Folk-Ballads of the English-speaking World,* ed. A. Friedman.) English and Scottish traditional ballads have been imitated by serious poets, especially since the early nineteenth century; probably the most famous of these **literary ballads** or **art ballads** are Coleridge's *Rime of the Ancient Mariner* and Keats's "La Belle Dame sans Merci." A **broadside ballad** was a poem of any sort printed on a large sheet (a broadside) and hawked by street singers in the sixteenth century. A. Rodway, in *Essays in Criticism,* 11 (1961), 215, summarizes the chief distinctions between the traditional ballad and the broadside or street ballad: "The traditional ballad tends to be rural, dramatic, heroic and inclined to the supernatural, the street ballad to be urban, reportative, debunking and inclined to realism." The folksong, Rodway adds, tends "to be rural, simple, amoral and inclined to pagan fertility feelings." Not until the eighteenth century was "ballad" limited to a traditional narrative song.

ballad stanza. See °ballad and °versification.

bard. Celtic for the poet who, in the British Isles in prefeudal times, composed and sang poems (chiefly °eulogies and °satires) to the warriors, who were the ruling class. Usually a warrior himself, he was an honored member of his society. The **scop** was the Old English name for the poet who sang oral poetry in England.

baroque. First used, in the eighteenth century, pejoratively, to describe a kind of architecture that flourished throughout the seventeenth century. The word has increasingly lost its pejorative tone, and has come to denote a style whose chief characteristic is a degree of explosive elaboration which almost obscures the underlying order or pattern: there is elaborate balance, but also a decided sense of strain or contortion. C. J. Friedrich (in *Horizon,* July 1960) says the characteristics are intensity, tension, conflicts, and extremes. He stresses the influence of (1) the Copernican system (which called to man's attention both his littleness and also the great power of science which could tell him about so enormous a world), and (2) the rise of great bureaucracies and empires (which called to man's attention the fact of feudal decay and the transiency of greatness). Baroque figures include Rubens, Rembrandt, Bach, Handel, and, among writers, Corneille and Crashaw. Applied to literature, the term is of uncertain meaning, sometimes honorific and sometimes pejorative. Douglas Bush aptly says (in *English Literature of the Earlier Seventeenth Century*): "The simplest definition is 'poetry like Crashaw's.' Its motto might be 'Over-ripeness is all.' " (For the structure of a baroque sentence, see °style. For a summary of theories, with bibliography, consult G. Highet, *The Classical Tradition;* R. Wellek, *Concepts of Criticism;* L. Nelson, *Baroque Lyric Poetry;* also, W. Sypher, *Four Stages of Renaissance Style.*)

bathos. See °pathos.

beast epic. A series of related tales about animals, often with °allegorical and °satiric implications. Reynard the Fox is the best known character. Such tales, especially popular in the Middle Ages, are as old as the fables attributed to Aesop (sixth century B.C.). (On beast epics consult W. T. H. Jackson, *The Literature of the Middle Ages.*) A single tale, such as Chaucer's "Nun's Priest's Tale," is a **beast fable.** The **bestiary** was not a satiric tale, but a collection of pious medieval allegorical interpretations of the animal world. For example, the phoenix, an alleged immortal bird that consumed itself in flames periodically and rose anew, was taken to represent the immortal resurrected soul.

Beat Generation. A rather disparate group of American writers (chiefly poets) of the 1950's and later, including Allen Ginsberg, Gregory Corso, Jack Kerouac, Lawrence Ferlinghetti, and Gary Snyder, most of whom share some of the following characteristics: residence in San Francisco; publication in *Evergreen Review;* an anti-rational bias that manifests itself in vatic, Whitmanesque utterance, in an interest in Zen Buddhism, and in experimentation with drugs; sympathy for the dispossessed (blacks, hoboes, drug addicts); pacificism and a belief that American society is in a very bad way; lines that are clear even when recited or sung. The term "beat" is variously explained as derived from "beaten up," "musical beat," and "beatific." (Consult *The Beats,* ed. S. Krim, and *A Casebook on the Beat,* ed. T. Parkinson.)

bestiary. See °beast epic.

bibliography. (1) "Enumerative bibliography" is a list of writings arranged according to some system, usually on a particular subject; or (2) "Analytic bibliography" is the art or science of accurately describing the physical properties of books. In this second sense, it is a highly technical procedure, requiring detailed knowledge of printers' methods. (Consult R. B. McKerrow, *An Introduction to Bibliography.*)

Bildungsroman. See °novel.

biography. Today, a detailed history of an individual (though lately there have been "biographies" of the ocean, the earth, and the film industry). Because a biographer must adhere to the facts, he is sometimes regarded (in Virginia Woolf's words) as a "craftsman, not an artist." Most Greek biographers were less concerned with presenting historical facts and detailed accounts than with presenting a clearly defined character, though Plutarch, the greatest ancient biographer, in his *Parallel Lives,* gives not mere eulogies but abundant concrete details about illustrious Greeks and Romans. Still, Plutarch admitted that he selected his details in an effort to reveal the essential character of his subject, and thus he was as much a literary man as a historian. Medieval biography is mostly the writing of saints' lives (**hagiography**); it emphasizes the piety of the subject without attempting to give all the details of his career. Fourteenth-century Italian biographers, however, wrote lives of various types of men, some unsaintly. The modern view of biography as the accurately detailed history of a man, with attention paid not only to his deeds but to his thoughts and his environment, developed in England in the eighteenth century, and flowered in Boswell's *Life of Johnson* (1791). An **autobiography** is the author's account of his own life; a **memoir** is the author's account not so much of himself as of the times he witnessed. (Consult L. Edel, *Literary Biography;* J. A. Garraty, *The Nature of Biography;* D. Stauffer's volumes on English biography through the eighteenth century; and R. Pascal, *Design and Truth in Autobiography.*)

blank verse. See °versification.

bombast. From a word meaning "cotton stuffing"; rant, speech that is too inflated for the occasion. At the end of Dryden's *Aureng-Zebe,* Nourmahal, who has swallowed poison, cries out before her death:

> I burn, I more than burn; I am all fire.
> See how my mouth and nostrils flame expire!
> I'll not come near myself –
> Now I'm a burning lake, it rolls and flows;
> I'll rush, and pour it all upon my foes.

bourgeois drama. A serious play with middle-class dramatis personae. There are a few Elizabethan tragedies of middle-class life, but bourgeois drama, with its emphasis on °pathos, is more or less an eighteenth-century invention. Bourgeois dramas were written in the eighteenth and nineteenth centuries, apparently in response to the middle class's desire to see itself on the stage; the bourgeois by the eighteenth century regarded himself as a suitable replacement for the nobleman of earlier tragedy. Speaking generally, the characteristics of these plays are: middle-class dramatis personae, virtue in distress, °sentimentality, and an unreasonably high moral tone. Eighteenth-century critics, not sure what to do with pathetic plays on middle-class life, used the terms *drame, drame bourgeois, comédie larmoyante* (tearful comedy), *tragédie bourgeoise,* and *bürgerliches Trauerspiel* (bourgeois tragedy) interchangeably. (Notice that a *comédie larmoyante* need not end happily, nor a *tragédie bourgeoise* end sadly.) In England, George Lillo's *The London Merchant* (1731), "a tale of private woe. A London 'prentice ruined," depicted an apprentice who murdered his benefactor. In France, Diderot compared *The London Merchant* to plays by Sophocles and Euripides. In Germany, it moved Lessing to write *Miss Sara Sampson* (1755), a play set in England: Sara, inveigled into eloping with a blackguard, is poisoned by his former mistress, causing him to repent his villainy in the presence of Sara's lamenting father. Unlike Miss Sara, bourgeois drama did not die in the eighteenth century; it lived on into the nineteenth century to become melodrama in many hands and tragedy in Ibsen's hands. (Consult Fred O. Nolte, *Early Middle Class Drama;* and Eric Auerbach, *Mimesis,* Ch. 17. On Ibsen as a bourgeois dramatist, consult Eric Bentley, *The Playwright as Thinker.*)

bowdlerize. A term derived from Dr. Thomas Bowdler (1754–1824), who edited *The Family Shakespeare* (first issued 1807), omitting "whatever is unfit to be read by a gentleman in the company of ladies." Though to bowdlerize is to delete sexual material, Bowdler also deleted "frivolous" references to the Bible. (Consult N. Perrin, *Dr. Bowdler's Legacy.*)

braggart soldier. The boastful, vain, cowardly soldier is a stock figure in much comedy. As a braggart, he belongs to the class *alazon* (see °convention). The ***miles gloriosus*** (plural: *milites gloriosi*), to give him his Latin name, in Roman comedies usually is in a position to buy the girl desired by the young lover; he is thus an obstacle to joy, but his cowardice makes him easily conquered. He is the *capitano* in the °*commedia dell'arte,* Shakespeare's Pistol (and even a part of Falstaff), and, by slight extension, Synge's Christy Mahon (who claims to have killed his father). (Consult D. Boughner, *The Braggart in Renaissance Comedy.*)

broadside ballad. See °ballad.

bucolic poetry. See °pastoral.

bull (or **Irish bull**). An unintentional juxtaposition of incongruous words or ideas, such as "Every man in the city, including women, greeted them," or "troops encircle the city, squaring with our strategy." Shakespeare's Julius Caesar says, "Caesar did never wrong but with just cause."

burlesque (or **caricature**). Any imitation of people or literature that, by distortion, aims to amuse. Its subject matter is sometimes said to be faults rather than vices, and its °tone is neither shrill nor savage. Thus, in distinction from °satire it can be defined as a comic imitation of a °mannerism or a minor fault (either in °style or subject-matter), contrived to arouse amusement rather than contempt and/or indignation. A **parody** (from the Greek "counter song") is a literary composition that imitates the °style (*e.g.*, meter, vocabulary, sentence-structure) of another work but normally substitutes a very different subject-matter. It amuses us, but need not make us devalue the original. The following lines from T. S. Eliot's "The Hollow Men":

> Between the conception
> And the creation
> Between the emotion
> And the response
> Falls the shadow;

are parodied in Myra Buttle's *Sweeniad:*

> Between the mustification
> And the deception
> Between the multiplication
> And the division
> Falls the Tower of London.

A **travesty,** or **low burlesque,** takes a lofty theme and treats it in trivial terms, as in the Greek *Battle of the Frogs and Mice,* which travesties Homer. A **mock-epic** or **mock-heroic** is a **high burlesque,** the reverse of a travesty, for it treats a trivial theme in a lofty style. It is a °narrative that, despite the name, does not mock the °epic, but mocks low or trivial activities by treating them in the elevated style of the epic. A comic effect results from the disparity between low subject and lofty treatment. Notice how by using a pyre, traditional in the epic, Pope's "Rape of the Lock" makes ridiculous the actions of a gentleman who

> to love an altar built,
> Of twelve vast French romances, neatly gilt.
> There lay three garters, half a pair of gloves;

And all the trophies of his former loves;
With tender billet-doux he lights the pyre,
And breathes three am'rous sighs to raise the fire.

In the theater, a burlesque may be a play that amusingly criticizes another play by grotesquely imitating aspects of it, as John Gay's *Beggar's Opera* mimicked serious operas, or, especially in England, a burlesque may be a musical extravaganza, or, especially in America, a sort of vaudeville or variety show stressing bawdy humor and sex. The sexual theme is most poignantly expressed in the strip-tease. (See °comedy and °satire. For collections of burlesques and parodies, see *The Antic Muse*, ed. R. P. Falk; *Twentieth-Century Parody*, ed. B. Lowrey; *Parodies*, ed. D. Macdonald. Consult also R. P. Bond, *English Burlesque Poetry, 1700–1750;* and V. C. Clinton-Baddeley, *The Burlesque Tradition in the English Theatre after 1660.*)

Byronic. See °classic.

cacophony. See °euphony.

caesura. See °versification.

canon. The undoubted works of a particular author or authors. Doubtful works are the **apocrypha.** Thus, most scholars include thirty-seven plays in the Shakespeare canon, but other plays, attributed to him on uncertain evidence, belong to the Shakespeare apocrypha. (Consult M. Chute, *Shakespeare of London,* Appendix 3.) Those books of the Bible officially recognized by a religious group as inspired constitute the canon; those rejected are the Apocrypha. (Consult *The Oxford Dictionary of the Christian Church,* ed. F. L. Cross.)

caricature. See °burlesque.

carol. Originally a circular dance or the song (usually of love) accompanying it; now, a Christmas song (in the Middle Ages it was customary to dance and sing around the Christmas crib) or a festive drinking song. (Consult E. Routley, *The English Carol.*)

Caroline. Adjective derived from Charles I of England (reigned 1625–42). "Caroline" can thus be applied to anything in the period, but it is frequently limited to literature produced by the **Cavalier poets,** courtly writers who supported the king against the °Puritans. Thus, although the Puritan Milton wrote during the Caroline period, he was not (in this second sense) a Caroline poet. Cavalier poets, such as Richard Lovelace and Sir John Suckling, wrote chiefly °lyrics of love, friendship, and gallant war, conveying a sense of cheerful manliness in the face of heavy outside pressures. Although not a courtier but a parson, Robert Herrick is usually grouped with these urbane writers. (Consult R. Skelton, ed., *The Cavalier Poets.*)

carpe diem. Latin phrase by Horace (65–8 B.C.), meaning "seize the day," *i.e.*, live for today. The most famous English presentation of this common °motif is perhaps Herrick's "To the Virgins, to Make Much of Time," which begins

> Gather ye rose-buds while ye may,
>   Old Time is still a-flying:
> And this same flower that smiles today,
>   To-morrow will be dying.

catalexis. See °versification.

catastrophe. See °plot.

catharsis. See °tragedy.

Cavalier poets. See °Caroline.

Celtic Renaissance. The creative outburst in Ireland late in the nineteenth century, continuing into the twentieth. William Butler Yeats and others sought to dignify Irish culture by producing art related to Irish life and traditions, but even James Joyce, who was unconcerned with dignifying Ireland, is considered part of the movement.

cesura. See °caesura (under °versification).

Chain of Being. See °Enlightenment.

character. (1) A literary form, consisting of a short sketch in prose or verse, not of an individual but of a type – *e.g.*, "the greedy man." Sometimes a "character" is imbedded in a longer work, say, an essay. Originated by Theophrastus (c. 372–c. 287 B.C.), the form was especially popular in England in the seventeenth century. (Consult G. Murphy, *A Cabinet of Characters;* B. Boyce, *The Theophrastian Character in England;* and M. Hodgart, *Satire,* pp. 163–68.) (2) A personage in a literary work. For this second sense, see °plot.

chiasmus, from the shape of the Greek letter X (*chi*). The second of two syntactically parallel phrases reverses the order of the first. Two examples are "Poor as a widow, as a widower cold," and "A fop their passion, but their prize a sot."

chorus. In Greek °drama, a group of twelve or fifteen performers who sang and danced during various parts of the play. The chorus sometimes functioned as a character; by representing common humanity, it often stood as a °foil to the hero. °Elizabethan dramas occasionally had a chorus of one actor who, not a participant in the story, commented on it. For example, the Chorus in Shakespeare's *Henry* V urges the audience to

> Think when we talk of horses that you see them
> Printing their proud hoofs i' the receiving earth;
> For 'tis your thoughts that now must deck our kings,
> Carry them here and there, jumping o'er times,
> Turning the accomplishment of many years
> Into an hour-glass: for the which supply,
> Admit me Chorus to this history:
> Who prologue-like your humble patience pray,
> Gently to hear, kindly to judge, our play.

A **chorus character** (or ***raisonneur***), however, such as Enobarbus in *Antony and Cleopatra,* is a character who participates in the story yet seems to express the attitude that the spectator is to hold. But Alfred Harbage, in *As They Liked It,* skeptically and aptly calls such a figure "The Unreliable Spokesman."

Christian humanism. See °Renaissance.

chronicle. A register of facts, in order of their occurrence; a history. The °Elizabethan **chronicle play,** popular around the end of the sixteenth century, dramatized historical material – or material thought to be historical – for a public anxious to see its past. The line is vague between a °tragedy with historical figures (Shakespeare's *Richard II*) and a chronicle play with tragic happenings, but, speaking broadly, tragedies show more concern with moral evil and less concern with political situations, than do chronicle plays. (See I. Ribner, *The Elizabethan History Play in the Age of Shakespeare;* and E. M. W. Tillyard, *Shakespeare's History Plays.*)

Ciceronian sentence. See °style.

cinéma vérité. See °documentary.

circumlocution. See °periphrasis.

classic and **romantic.** For the Romans of the second century A.D., **classic** meant "a first-class author." For the Middle Ages and the °Renaissance, it meant "a writer read in the classroom," *i.e.*, an ancient author, not necessarily first-class. Today it may not only mean "first-class" and "ancient," but also "typical," as when physicians speak of a classic case of measles. **Romantic** is from a medieval Latin adverb, *romanice; scribere romanice* means "to write in *lingua Romanica,*" a vernacular language derived from

Latin. A tale written in the vernacular was a *roman*, and, because such a tale was frequently filled with unexpected improbable happenings, "romantic" came, by the middle of the seventeenth century, to mean "improbable." In the eighteenth century the word's meanings ranged from "silly" to "highly appealing to the imagination."

The two words, "classic" and "romantic," are now sometimes applied to contrasting attitudes: the classical mind delights in the probable or typical, the unified, the static, the finite. The romantic mind delights in the improbable, the varied, the dynamic, the infinite. The contrast has sometimes been illustrated by comparing a Greek temple (allegedly simple, orderly, built according to strict rules) with a Gothic cathedral (allegedly elaborate, asymmetrical, built largely as the spirit moved the builders, and aspiring toward the heavens). T. S. Eliot, an avowed classicist, says in "The Function of Criticism" that the difference "seems to me rather the difference between the complete and the fragmentary, the adult and the immature, the orderly and the chaotic." In Europe, those authors of the seventeenth and eighteenth centuries who looked respectfully to ancient models, assuming that the ancients had attained an excellence which later (medieval) writers had not remotely equalled, are called **neoclassicists** (*i.e.*, new classicists). From the works of the past certain rules were abstracted concerning the choice of words (see °decorum), plots (see under °unity, °Three Unities), etc. The neoclassical author, such as Racine, Voltaire, Addison, or Pope, assumed that literature was the product of careful study, study not only of the world around him but of the past, and he sought to correct any local bias by looking back to Greece and especially to Rome. Here is Pope's advice to the literary critic:

> Be Homer's works your study and delight,
> Read them by day, and meditate by night;
> Thence form your judgment, thence your maxims bring,
> And trace the muses upward to their spring.

The neoclassicist thus repressed personal views (in theory, at least) and subjected his mind to the correction of all society, past and present. In practice, much of the best English neoclassical literature is by Pope and Swift, self-assured satirists who were extremely dissatisfied with the opinions and deeds of many members of their society. But in their assumption that men of their time had fallen from virtue and should be recalled to ancient standards, Pope and Swift represent neoclassical respect for antiquity and for discipline.

The later eighteenth century saw the rise of a **Romantic**

Movement, a reaction against what was thought to be a sterile debasing of the ancients by unimaginative men who pretended to be artists but were mere copyists and thinkers, not feelers. The romantics had great respect for the "classics" in the sense of "ancient writers," but unlike the neoclassicists they did not often imitate them closely. The neoclassical writer, regarding art as the °imitation of nature, was proud of his craftsmanship; the romantic writer, regarding art as (in Wordsworth's formula) "the spontaneous overflow of powerful feelings," valued deep feeling. Byron (a romantic who admired Pope and despised most romantics) claimed he did not bother to revise his work: "I am like a tiger: if I miss my first spring, I go grumbling back to my jungle." The romantic, valuing originality, spontaneity, and the individual and his development (rather than the stable group), asserted his own personality. Pope wrote an "Essay on Man" — man in general; Wordsworth wrote mostly about himself. Here is a part of Wordsworth's Preface to his autobiographical poem, *The Prelude:*

> Several years ago, when the Author retired to his native mountains, with the hope of being enabled to construct a literary work that might live, it was reasonable that he should take a review of his own mind, and examine how far Nature and Education had qualified him for such employment. As subsidiary to this preparation, he undertook to record, in verse, the origin and progress of his own powers.

This romantic preoccupation with oneself (especially evident in °lyric poetry, which in the Romantic Age became a major genre) enlarged the subject-matter of literature, for the writer delved into his private inner world, a world of strong personal feelings. As Coleridge says in his *Biographia Literaria,* there are men who "venture at times into the twilight realms of consciousness, and . . . feel a deep interest in modes of inmost being." Such turning inward meant that the romantic poet often took himself as his hero. Where the ancient °bard sang of the warrior, and was thus a poet singing to society about its champions, the romantic poet sometimes withdrew from society to brood upon himself, and to cheer himself with solitary song. The **Byronic hero** (named for characteristics found in many of the heroes of Byron's poetry) stood apart from men; sometimes he was an outlaw, but always he felt outlawed. He was bold, a defiant champion of liberty (Byron himself died fighting for Greek freedom), but moody and sensitive, feeling the world

> a place of agony and strife
> Where, for some sin, to sorrow I was cast,
> To act and suffer.

(*Childe Harold's Pilgrimage*)

His boldness and defiance, frustrated by a tyrannical world, turned in upon the hero himself, and he gnawed his heart with melancholy, yet apparently enjoyed his pain. In short, the Byronic hero was pleased to regard himself as a stricken eagle. (This point will be continued, later in this entry, in the comments on *le poète maudit*. Consult P. Thorslev, *The Byronic Hero*.)

It must be remembered, however, that if Byronism is romantic, not all romanticism is Byronic. Byronism perhaps may be said to be the romantic cult of inwardness gone sour, yet still affording masochistic pleasure. The romantic search for subjects other than the materialistic world led not only to a journey inward upon the self, but to other areas that the neoclassicists had neglected. Where the neoclassicists had written of mature men, the romantic often wrote about personal development, and therefore about childhood. Some romantics held that the child felt, the man merely thought; the child's intuitive wisdom was gradually obliterated by the intellect, which knew only one kind of truth. Akin to the romantic interest in childhood was the romantic interest in childlike people – simple shepherds, for example, who allegedly preserved the powers nature gave them at their birth. (See °primitivism.) This interest was extended even to animals, flowers, and inanimate objects; in an extreme moment Wordsworth could say:

> One impulse from a vernal wood
> May teach you more of man,
> Of moral evil and of good,
> Than all the sages can. ("The Tables Turned")

For the neoclassicists, man learned from man, not from vernal woods. Indeed, the woods scarcely existed for neoclassicists, "nature" for them meaning something like "human nature" or "cosmic law," as in the expression "law of nature." But external nature was important to the romantics: when a stranger visited Wordsworth's house, a servant showed him about; asked where the study was, the servant took the stranger to the library and said, "This is master's library, but he studies in the fields." Notice, however, that romantic "nature poems" are, more often than not, meditations on an emotional situation, rather than mere descriptions of external nature.

The romantic interest in the child and the childlike extended to cultures that the neoclassicists had neglected. The Middle Ages, scorned by the neoclassicists as immature, provided the background for some impressive romantic works, notably Coleridge's "Christabel" and Keats's "Eve of St. Agnes." There is a shift of interest (with a corresponding shift in °diction) from urban and civilized to rural and naive. This taste for the unsophisticated, the remote, the fantastic was sometimes escapist, but it was sometimes a vehicle for the communication of spiritual insights to an age that worshipped machines and facts. The poet voyaged in his "strange seas of thought, alone" (Wordsworth's phrase) and found a realm more important than the industrial age in which most men lived. But the poet who perceived a new world sometimes found himself painfully apart from the men of the ordinary world. True, for Wordsworth the poet was "a man speaking to men," differing from them only in his greater power of sensibility and of expression, but for some romantics the gap was enormous. Shelley considered himself a "weak and sensitive nature" surrounded by a "hellish society of men." The romantic poet's sensitivity, such poets sometimes held, made him an outcast from the world of crasser men, and the gift of imagination made the poet accursed (***le poète maudit***).

The distinctions between neoclassicism and romanticism are not, of course, so clear-cut in practice. Pope, for example, emphasizes unity in his theory, but in practice many of his works are only loosely unified. And although Keats was a romantic in his stress on spontaneity ("if Poetry comes not as naturally as the Leaves to a tree it had better not come at all"), he was in fact a painstaking reviser of his work. Still, there is a difference between a neoclassicist and a romantic. As René Wellek has suggested in an important essay in his *Concepts of Criticism* (especially pp. 160–92), the romantics (1) view nature not as a machine but as something growing and infused with what Wordsworth called "a sense sublime"; (2) view poetry as imagination; and (3) employ °symbol and °myth. That is, for the romantics nature is alive with deity, and is understood by the imagination rather than by dispassionate reason; "the shaping spirit of imagination," as Coleridge called it, presents in literature not a mere copy but a significant myth – what Blake called a "Divine Vision." (See °Apollonian, °Augustan, °diction, °Enlightenment, °lyric, °ode. Consult I. Babbitt, *Rousseau and Romanticism* [anti-romantic]; J. Barzun, *Romanticism and the Modern Ego* [pro-romantic]; G. Highet, *The Classical Tradition;* H. Hugo, *The Romantic Reader;* L. R. Furst, *Romanticism in Perspective;* H. Bloom, ed., *Romanticism and Consciousness;* and, for an account of romantic critical theory, M. H. Abrams, *The Mirror and the Lamp*.)

cliché. A stale phrase used where a fresh one is needed. The trouble with such old phrases is in their suggestion of unimaginativeness and imprecision. The writer who describes "the blushing bride" as "a clinging vine" uses clichés, inadvertently letting us know that he is unimaginative in contexts calling for imagination. He bores rather than interests his reader. Some phrases once exciting (Shakespeare's "Something is rotten in the state of Denmark") have, through repeated use, become clichés. Notice, however, that "How do you do?" is not a cliché, for it adequately serves its purpose.

climax. See °plot.

closed couplet. See °versification.

close-up. See °shot.

cognitive meaning. See °connotation.

comedy. Most broadly, anything amusing – a literary work or a situation – is a comedy. More specifically, comedy is a kind of °drama wherein the audience is amused. Dramatic comedies generally depict a movement from unhappiness to happiness, from (for example) young lovers frustrated by their parents to young lovers happily married. The unhappy situation is so presented that it entertains rather than distresses the spectator; it is ridiculous and/or diverting rather than painful.

Comic drama seems related to fertility °rituals; it generally celebrates generation, renewal, variety (laughing away any narrow-minded persons who seek to limit life's abundance), and it celebrates man's triumphs over the chances of life. Irate parents and shipwrecks cannot prevent journeys from ending with lovers meeting. Greek comedy (from *comos,* Greek for "revel") is usually divided into Old Comedy, Middle Comedy, and New Comedy. **Old Comedy,** exemplified by Aristophanes (448?–380? B.C.), combines fantastic elements (*e.g.*, a °utopia founded by birds) with raucous political °satire. Essentially it is a series of conflicts or verbal contests (a contest is an ***agon***), rather like a vaudeville show, with characters coming and going without much relation to a continuous and evolving story. It usually concludes with expressions of joy, after the obstreperous people have been hooted out. No Middle Comedy survives, but it seems to have been transitional to **New Comedy** – exemplified by Menander (343?–291? B.C.) – which has a plot that works toward an end. Usually it is of the boy-meets-girl sort, often combining adventure with scenes of ordinary life; there are obstacles to a union, but finally the lovers are brought together. The ending suggests sexual fulfillment and, more generally, a sense of renewed individuals and a renewed society. The basic formula of New Comedy was continued in Rome by Plautus (254?–184 B.C.) and Terence (190?–159? B.C.). (On the characters in classical comedy, see

°convention. Consult K. Lever, *The Art of Greek Comedy.* On Old and New Comedy, today as well as in ancient Greece, see N. Frye, *Shakespeare Survey* 22.)

Most comedies since the °Renaissance fall roughly into three sorts: (1) **romantic comedies,** such as most of Shakespeare's, in which the stage-world is a delightful never-never land (Illyria, The Forest of Arden) and the chief figures are lovers; (2) **critical** or **satiric comedies,** such as Molière's, in which the chief figures, who often interfere with the lovers, are ridiculed; and (3) **rogue comedies,** such as Jonson's *Alchemist,* in which the chief figures are pleasant scoundrels who, by outwitting their less astute neighbors, entertain us, perhaps because they represent a fulfillment of our rebellious instincts. All three of these commonly use the basic formula of New Comedy, but the second and third do not put the emphasis on the lovers who are working toward fulfillment. **Comedy of humors** is a term sometimes applied to plays – notably those of Ben Jonson – wherein the characters, though somewhat individualized, obviously represent types or moods (the jealous husband, the witless pedant). A humor was a bodily liquid (blood, phlegm, yellow bile, black bile) thought to control one's behavior. Allegedly, a proper mixture produced a well-adjusted man, but a preponderance of any one humor produced a distorted personality. For Jonson this abnormal psychological condition has moral implications, the character being not merely sick but immoral. (See J. Redwine, ed., *Ben Jonson's Literary Criticism,* pp. xxiv–xxix.) The old sense of the word survives in the phrase, "He is in a bad humor"; "sanguine," "choleric," "phlegmatic," and "bilious" are also modern survivals of the old psychology of humors. **Humor characters** are common in **situational comedy;** the characters are engineered by a clever plot into a situation that displays their absurdity: the man who craves silence is confronted with a talkative woman; the coward is confronted by the braggart; the hypochondriacal lady meets a veterinarian and asks for medical advice. **Farce** is a sort of comedy based not on clever language or subtleties of character, but on broadly humorous situations (a man mistakenly enters the ladies' locker room). It usually is full of surprises, improbabilities, complications, and speed, plot outdistancing characterization. E. Bentley, in his introduction to *"Let's Get a Divorce" and Other Plays,* suggests that like dreams, farce shows "the disguised fulfillment of repressed wishes." **Slapstick** (named for an implement made of two slats which resound when slapped against a posterior) is farce that relies on physical assault.

At the other extreme from **low comedy** is **high comedy;** intellectual rather than physical, it requires the close attention of a sophisticated audience. Etherege, Wycherley, Congreve, and other playwrights of the decades immediately following the °Restoration of Charles II to the throne of England (1660) wrote **Restoration comedy** of a particular sort, often called **comedy of manners** or **comedy of wit.** Their plays abound in witty **repartee** (what Dr. Johnson called "gay remarks and unexpected answers"), and often strike modern audiences as cynical. The following example is from Congreve's *The Way of the World* (1700): "Marriage is honorable, as you say; and if so, wherefore should cuckoldom be a discredit, being derived from so honorable a root?" The common assumption in much comedy of wit, that love, marriage, and conventional notions of romance are humbug, caused George Meredith, in his *An Essay on Comedy* (1877), to speak of "our so-called Comedy of Manners, or Comedy of the manners of South-Sea Islanders under city veneer." Recently, however, it has been seen that the Restoration dramatists were not merely flippant and without values, but were forcefully presenting a view of man as selfish, pleasure-loving, and skeptical of traditions that could not withstand the scrutiny of reason. Furthermore, in *The Way of the World,* Congreve °satirizes the "affected wit" of most of his characters, and rejects the view that love is a fiction. Restoration comedy (which has no precise terminal date) can be said to end about 1700, when satire came to be directed against heartless cleverness rather than against deviations from manners. Coincident with the decline of comedy of manners is the development of °sentimental comedy. (Consult H. T. E. Perry, *Masters of Dramatic Comedy;* T. H. Fujimura, *The Restoration Comedy of Wit;* L. Kronenberger, *The Thread of Laughter;* and N. N. Holland, *The First Modern Comedies.*)

Comedy in the sense of the laughable has been the subject of innumerable analyses. One common distinction is that between wit and humor. **Wit,** from an Old English word meaning "mind," "reason," "intelligence," has had several meanings, but behind them there is usually the shadow of John Locke's definition: "The assemblage of ideas, and putting those together with quickness and variety." Thus, in the court of Charles II, a wit was an intellectual. C. S. Lewis points out, in *Studies in Words,* that by the first half of the seventeenth century "wit" commonly meant sprightly language rather than good sense. "Wit" was, however, often variously used even by a single author, especially in the eighteenth century. Pope, in his "Essay on Criticism," speaks of works that are "one glaring chaos and wild heap of wit," "wit" meaning something like fanciful imagination as opposed to judgment. But Pope also says, "True wit is nature to advantage dressed, / What oft was thought, but ne'er so well express'd," "wit" meaning something like felicitously phrased common ideas which are true, or, in short, good sense. Later in the eighteenth century Dr. Johnson took issue with Pope's second definition, and defined "wit" as "that which though not obvious is, upon its first production, acknowledged to be just." "Wit" has come, however, to be associated particularly with one variety of cleverness; it is no longer merely Locke's quick assemblage of ideas, but an assemblage that, by its striking observation and phraseology – usually compressed and mocking – evokes laughter or amusement. (See "comedy of wit," above; but for another meaning of "wit," see °irony.) In short, wit today commonly means clever raillery. Often contrasted with comic wit – and with °satire, for satire like comic wit is aggressive – is **humor.** In this sense, humor is genial, joshing at eccentricities, including one's own. George Meredith says in *An Essay on Comedy*, "If you laugh all round him [*i.e.*, a ridiculous person], tumble him, roll him about, deal him a smack, and drop a tear on him, own his likeness to you, and yours to your neighbor, spare him as little as you shun, pity him as much as you expose, it is a spirit of Humor that is moving you." Saroyan is a humorist, then, and so are Kaufman and Hart in *You Can't Take It with You*. Sometimes wit is said to be the perception of resemblances, humor the perception of incongruities. In short, most usage suggests that wit involves intellectual agility, humor involves sympathy. (For "comedy of humors," see above.) Sigmund Freud, in "Wit and Its Relation to the Unconscious" (reprinted in the Modern Library's *Basic Writings of Sigmund Freud*), distinguishes between wit (twenty-three varieties), humor, and comedy, but these distinctions have gained little currency among literary critics. (Freud's essay is difficult, and the student will be aided by D. H. Monro's analysis of it in *The Argument of Laughter*.)

Theories analyzing the laughable as a whole commonly fall into one of two categories: (1) laughter is evoked by (in Hobbes's famous phrase) "a kind of sudden glory," wherein the spectator abruptly perceives his superiority to others, as when he sees the awkward posture of someone who slips on a banana peel; (2) laughter is evoked by (in Kant's famous phrase) a "transformation of a strained expectation into nothing," as when we laugh at the comedian who says "I have enough money to last me the rest of my life – provided I die a week from Tuesday." In this second example the alleged humor consists in a statement that causes us abruptly to release the tension we generate thinking that we are in the presence of a wealthy man. (See °burlesque and °satire. Consult L. J. Potts, *Comedy;* T. M. Parrott, *Shakespearean*

Comedy; Albert Cook, *The Dark Voyage and the Golden Mean;* D. H. Monro, *The Argument of Laughter;* and W. K. Wimsatt, Jr., and C. Brooks, *Literary Criticism: A Short History.*)

comic relief. Humorous episodes in °tragedy, alleged to alleviate or lighten the tragic effect. Some comic scenes in tragedy, however, not only provide "relief" but enlarge the canvas of tragedy, showing us a fuller picture of life. The clown who brings Cleopatra the poisonous asp sets her tragedy against the daily world. Critics have increasingly noted that in some of the greatest tragedies the comic scenes (such as the macabre comments of the grave-digger in *Hamlet*) often deepen rather than alleviate the tragic effect. (See °tragicomedy. Consult A. P. Rossiter, *Angel with Horns,* Ch. 14.)

commedia dell'arte. Dramatic °comedy employing °stock characters, performed (especially in the sixteenth century) by professional Italian actors, who improvised while they performed. A sketch of the plot (*scenario*) specified exits and entrances, but the plot was fleshed out with improvisations upon stock bits of comic business (*lazii;* singular: *lazzo*), such as the *lazzo* of anger. Among the characters were the Merchant (Pantalone), the Doctor (Graziano), some young lovers, a clever servant (Arlecchino), and a stupid servant (Pulcinella). (Consult A. Nicoll, *Masks, Mimes and Miracles;* and K. M. Lea, *Italian Popular Comedy.*)

Commonwealth. See °Puritan Interregnum.

complaint. See °lyric.

complication. See °plot.

conceit. See °metaphysical poets.

concrete and **abstract.** These words and certain related ones are fairly clear in their primary usage, but when extended to whole literary works, they become rather obscure. The **concrete** is the existent, in all its rich complexity and uniqueness. It can be reached for by accumulating precise description. So, many say that the more detailed, specific, and complete a description is, the more "concrete" it is. Thus, they would hold, "this book of Shakespeare's plays, consisting of 928 pages" is more concrete than "this book of Shakespeare's plays." There are several kinds of **abstract** entities, all of which are either other than or "thinner" than the objects of the concrete world. Numbers, and ideals like justice, purity, and perhaps representative government, are abstract entities that some people think "subsist" in another realm than the concrete. Classes (*i.e.*, groups of things similar in some respect, which are referred to and considered in virtue of that respect) are another sort of abstract entity. Examples are mankind, cities of over 10,000, United States citizens, antiques. Another kind of abstract entity is attributes (also called characteristics or qualities), such as colors, shapes, sizes, etc. – any trait that can be *abstracted from* a concrete thing, but cannot exist by itself. A passage may be called "abstract" when it deals with any of the several sorts of abstract entities named, or else, if in a literary work, it falls short of a rich concrete presentation. Thus a story of a crime and its effects on the criminal might be called abstract to the extent that it omits his motivation.

Two terms that form an overlapping classification with concrete and abstract are **particular** and **universal.** The universal is in principal repeatable – the color of a bluejay, a lake, and a pair of eyes is one universal, blue – and the particular is unrepeatable, unique. Literary critics call a subject or theme of a work "universal" when the work portrays an experience common to all men (*e.g.*, death) or, more loosely, when it portrays an experience or a characteristic common to most men (*e.g.*, ambition) or to all men in varying degrees (*e.g.*, love, intelligence).

Another pair of terms is applied not at all to kinds of beings in the world, but only to kinds of words. These are **singular** and **general.** A singular term applies only to one thing; a general term applies to many things. Proper names are perfect examples of singular terms. General terms apply to more or fewer things, and often can be arranged in hierarchies of generality: "bluejay," "bird," "vertebrate." In reference to passages rather than words, a correct pair of alternatives is perhaps "specific" and "general." The admonition, "Be specific," does not mean "Be concrete," for one may talk very specifically about the number seven, the color blue, or special income tax requirements, or one may discuss something in concrete detail but leave out those details that make it unique, and so pin one's subject down by its repeatable characteristics rather than by name, time, or place. However, the admonitions, "Be concrete" and "Be specific," may of course be combined.

Literary theorists have tended to stress either "concreteness" or "universality" or both as the proper goal of literature. W. K. Wimsatt, Jr., in *The Verbal Icon,* attempts to combine the two in his theory of the **concrete universal,** for which he points out precedents in Aristotle, Plotinus, Hegel, and others. The theory is, roughly, that literature gives representations that are "very concrete," have considerable and precise detail and specificity; but these represented concrete particulars *stand for* much else, and herein lies their generality or "universality." A great work (Sophocles's *King Oedipus*) portrays a particular thing concretely

(Oedipus, King of Thebes), which thing in turn is a °symbol for much else besides (man's tragic search for self-knowledge). Wimsatt suggests that the "very concrete" and yet also "universal" character of literature comes especially from the *connection* of the details set forth, a unique presentational connection, which yet is superbly representative of otherwise inexpressible real facts that are important to us. Good technique is the achievement of this difficult revelatory presentation. Thus the careful analysis of literary technique not only shows us how art does its work, but also brings us to a fuller appreciation of its achievement.

concrete poetry. Poetry that is not so much read as looked at: punctuation marks or letters or words (if words, usually they are orthographically similar, such as NET and NIT) are arranged on a page to form a visual design. The poem is not usually syntactical and it may be looked at from bottom to top, from right to left, or from top left to bottom right. (Consult *Beloit Poetry Journal*, 17 [Fall 1966]; M. R. Rosenthal, *The New Poets;* and M. E. Solt, *Concrete Poetry*.)

confidant (feminine: **confidante**). A character in whom a principal character confides, revealing his state of mind and often furthering the °exposition (see under °plot). Horatio is Hamlet's confidant; Oenone is Phèdre's. Although Horatio and Oenone are memorable, the confidant is sometimes absurdly vapid; and although the French defended the device as more plausible than the °soliloquy, the confidant may be more trouble than he is worth. In *The Critic* (1779), Sheridan ridiculed it thus: "Enter Tiburnia stark mad in white satin, and her confidante stark mad in white linen."

conflict. See °plot.

connotation and denotation. For literary critics, the **denotation** of a word is the dictionary definition, and the **connotations** are the suggestions or associations aroused. Thus, though the denotation of "cravat" and "necktie" is the same ("a decorated band worn under the collar, and knotted in front"), "cravat" connotes wealth, high fashion, perhaps stuffiness, etc. (It should be noted that philosophers define denotation and connotation differently; for them, the denotation of a word is the thing or things to which the word refers, and the connotation names particular attributes. Thus, "rational animal" and "featherless biped" both refer to man, but they have different connotations because they call attention to different properties of man.) The **emotive meaning** is the emotion in a speaker or hearer that is conventionally associated with the word. Thus, though the denotation of "cravat" is "a decorated band" and the connotation is "an expensive decorated band," the emotive meaning includes (for example) the sense of irritation that a malcontent may feel as a result of the connotations. Emotive meaning is contrasted with **cognitive meaning.** Assertions about reality (such as "two plus two equals four") have cognitive (also called "referential" and "descriptive") meaning. Purely cognitive statements supposedly do not express the speaker's attitude or emotion. At the other extreme is purely emotive meaning; "ouch," "gee," "ha ha" communicate or induce an emotional state rather than assert any proposition about reality. "Shakespeare died in 1616" is cognitive (so, indeed, is "Shakespeare died in 1700," which is false); but Milton's lines in "L'Allegro" expressing delight in hearing "sweetest Shakespeare, Fancy's child, / Warble his native wood-notes wild," are largely emotive, for Milton is in large part giving vent to his attitude toward Shakespeare, that is, he is expressing his own state of mind. I. A. Richards holds, in *The Principles of Literary Criticism,* that poetry has not cognitive but emotive meaning, and is a sort of splendid version of such emotional gestures as stamping, clapping, and shrugging. He holds that poetry is therefore neither true nor false, for it does not make assertions but only expresses and arouses emotions. Keats's "A thing of beauty is a joy forever" is not (in the emotive view) an assertion that is right or wrong, but an expression of an emotion, and it is not valued for its truth but for its ability to organize the reader's emotions. (Consult M. C. Beardsley, *Aesthetics.*)

consonance. See °versification.

content. See °form.

convention. (1) In art, an unrealistic device that the public agrees to tolerate. Thus, Hamlet, though a Dane, speaks in English; and a character in a drama may express his thoughts aloud and not be heard by other characters on the stage (this device is an °aside), or he may speak his thoughts aloud on an empty stage (the °soliloquy). Similarly, the use of rhyme is a convention, for people do not commonly speak it. In motion pictures, one image fades out, another fades in, and through this convention the audience knows that there is a shift in time or place. Though such deviations from reality may sometimes be the result of the artist's inability to handle his material, they are more often the devices whereby art is made art and not a mere reproduction of reality. No one, for example, confuses rhymed discourse with real talk. Yet it is partly through the convention of rhyme that the poem or play has its value. (Consult H. Levin, *Refractions.*) (2)

More generally, any character-type, theme, °topic, or °motif (*e.g.*, tragic love in grand opera, the suspected butler in a detective story, love at first sight in any sort of writing) widely used in literary work is a convention. Conventional characters, called **stock characters,** are types that recur in numerous works. For example, from Greek comedy to the present there have been numerous °braggart soldiers, stubborn fathers; and jealous husbands. Northrop Frye finds four chief types of comic figures: (1) the *alazon* (impostor, boaster, hypocrite); (2) the *eiron* (the man who deprecates himself and exposes the boaster); (3) the *bomolochos* (buffoon, or, more generally, the man who entertains by his mannerisms and talk); and (4) *agroikos* (the straightman who is the unwitting butt of humor). Each of these types appears in many dresses; the *alazon,* for example, is most commonly the braggart soldier, but he is also the pedant, the crank, or anyone who is full of ideas that have no relation to reality. (Consult N. Frye, *Anatomy of Criticism*, pp. 171–76.) Stock characters are not, of course, limited to comedy: the proud tragic hero is a stock character, as are the cruel stepmother and the son who wishes to avenge his father. A **stock situation** is one common in literature, such as the separation by shipwreck of twins, as in Shakespeare's *Comedy of Errors* and *Twelfth Night.*

conversation poem. See °lyric.

couplet. See °versification.

courtly love. The idea, born in Provence in the eleventh century, that love (in contrast to mere sexual interest) is limited to the nobility. The lady's beauty strikes the man's heart painfully through the eye, and he undergoes such physical disturbances as loss of color and appetite; but if the lady responds, the lover regains his health, and serves her humbly and courteously, obedient to her every whim. Although in Chaucer's "Knight's Tale" Palamon's love for Emily leads to marriage, the system glorified extramarital sex (partly because medieval marriages were practical rather than romantic) on the theory that true love must be freely given and is therefore impossible between a husband and wife whose *duty* it is to love each other. Courtly love, though it involves fornication, was thought to be limited to persons of high moral potential. The love was dignified by rites which imitated religious rites: the lover "adored" his lady, and genuflected at her chamber door. Furthermore, strictly Christian behavior (in all respects other than this love) had to be observed. (Consult C. S. Lewis, *The Allegory of Love*; E. T. Donaldson, *Speaking of Chaucer*; and M. Valency, *In Praise of Love.*)

crisis. See °plot.

criticism. The art (or science) of criticizing. "To criticize" is, etymologically, "to judge," or, to go even further back, "to cut" or "to analyze." But the standards by which critics judge or cut or analyze vary greatly. **Impressionistic critics** hold that it is enough if the critic expresses his feelings, and that he need not analyze the work to see why the feelings are thus aroused. As William Hazlitt says, "In art, in taste, in life, in speech, you decide from feeling, and not from reason; that is, from the impression of a number of things on the mind, which impression is true and well-founded, though you may not be able to analyze or account for it in the several particulars." Emily Dickinson says, "If I read a book and it makes my body so cold no fire can ever warm me, I know that is poetry. If I feel physically as if the top of my head were taken off, I know that is poetry. These are the only ways I know it." Such criticism verges on autobiography, for the critic talks largely about his emotional reaction (and is therefore an **affective critic**), but he also passes judgment on the work, and may, even as Remy de Gourmont says any sincere man will do, "erect into laws his personal impressions." It is therefore unfortunate that critics who judge a work against allegedly enduring laws are sometimes distinguished by the term **judicial critics.** Judicial criticism seeks at least to be the product (as Henry James put it) "of opinion . . . that is capable of giving some intelligible account of itself." Such criticism engages in **analysis** – the examination of the parts and their relation to the whole. Analysis in itself is sometimes held to be criticism, but more often judgment is held to be indispensable to the critical performance. T. S. Eliot, in *The Use of Poetry and the Use of Criticism,* says that criticism is "that department of thought which either seeks to find out what poetry is . . . or . . . assesses actual poetry."

The **theoretical critic** is concerned with principles rather than with particular works, though like Aristotle he may touch on particular works. The **practical critic** is concerned with particular works – though he may in fact be examining particular works to see how well they conform to his general theory. (Consult I. A. Richards, *Practical Criticism.*) If a critic holds that there is only one right judgment, only one true verdict about a work of art, he is an **absolutist.** If he holds that values can change, and that a work may have been great for eighteenth-century Englishmen but is not great for twentieth-century Americans, he is a **relativist.** (For interesting relativist criticism consult F. A. Pottle, *The Idiom of Poetry.*) Note that the relativist may argue with others about views. He may hold that persons of, say, the same cultural environment and the same psychological make-up ought to agree in evaluating works; but he will not insist that his view is true for eternity. If a critic holds that preferences are unarguable (as most impressionistic critics do), he is a **subjectivist.**

Numerous adjectives have been affixed to "criticism," denoting particular schools. **Marxist criticism** varies with the party line, but usually explains literature in terms of the kind of society that produced it, holding with Leon Trotsky (though not with Marx himself) that "Marxism alone can explain why and how a given tendency in art has originated in a given period in history." Marxism often judges a literary work by the attitude it displays toward classes or by its ability to hold the attention of the proletariat. Thus, some Marxists have praised Shakespeare for depicting tyrannical noblemen and honest workmen or for interesting the ordinary laborer, while other Marxists have denounced him for his unflattering depictions of ignorant plebians and his contemptuous references to the groundlings who paid only a penny to see his plays. A **Freudian critic** is in some measure a follower of Freud; he generally praises a work to the degree to which it recognizes the things (*e.g.*, the Oedipus complex) that Freud recognized. Freudian criticism often veers into biography, finding in the literary work clues to the author's personality, and explaining the work in terms of the occurrences in the author's childhood. (An interesting example is Van Wyck Brooks's *The Ordeal of Mark Twain.* For a survey of Marxist and Freudian criticism, consult S. E. Hyman, *The Armed Vision;* on Freud, consult L. Trilling, *The Liberal Imagination.*)

The **textual critic,** perhaps better called the "textual scholar," seeks to establish the proper text for study, and he thus must decide by knowledge (often of printing-house procedures) and reasoning whether, for example, Hamlet wished (according to the various printed texts) his "solid flesh" or "sullied flesh" or "sallied flesh" to melt. (Consult F. Bowers, *Textual and Literary Criticism.*) "Textual criticism," in an entirely different sense, has occasionally referred to the **new criticism,** a school whose name was probably fixed by John Crowe Ransom's book, *The New Criticism* (1941). "New criticism" is commonly applied to the methods practiced notably by Cleanth Brooks, Robert Penn Warren, Allen Tate, R. P. Blackmur, and Ransom himself – and sometimes by I. A. Richards, to some of whose writings these other men are indebted. Broadly, the new critics (deeply indebted to Coleridge and T. S. Eliot) hold that literature is not to be judged as ethics, science, theology, history, etc.; criticism is an act of analyzing and evaluating a work of literature, and is not concerned with the perceiver's emotional reaction (here they differ from

I. A. Richards), or with the biography of the writer, or with the influence of the work on later history. Cleanth Brooks points out, in *The Kenyon Review*, 13 (Winter 1951), that although Hemingway reportedly considered *Across the River and into the Trees* his best novel, this statement is of interest to the biographer but not to the critic. Furthermore, the new critics in studying a piece of literature concentrate on the language of the piece (the old art of °explication) rather than on any alleged overall structure independent of the words. Thus, they do not begin an analysis of Gray's "Elegy" by discussing the °elegy as a traditional form of literature with a particular purpose and with certain devices appropriate to it; rather, they study the words in the poem and find the form in the total pattern of the language. They tend to place a high value on °paradox and °irony, preferring poetry (such as that of the °metaphysicals, *e.g.*, John Donne) that has a good deal of complexity. The chief attacks on new criticism hold that it is too little concerned with the ethical content of literature, too arbitrary in its emphasis on complexity, and too preoccupied with individual words. Among the chief opponents of the new critics are the **historical critics**, who assume the relevance of the literary tradition in which an author writes, as well as of his biography and social milieu. Generally the historical critic is a relativist. One can conveniently see some of the contrasting approaches of new critics (*e.g.*, Brooks) and historical critics (*e.g.*, Douglas Bush) in the varying interpretations of Marvell's "An Horatian Ode," in *The Sewanee Review*, 55 (Spring 1947); 60 (Summer 1952); 61 (Winter 1953).

(An excellent anthology of criticism [Greeks to the present] is W. J. Bate, *Criticism: The Major Texts*. For a history covering the whole field, consult W. K. Wimsatt, Jr., and C. Brooks, *Literary Criticism: A Short History*. For a history of Greek, Latin, and English criticism through the eighteenth century, consult J. W. Atkins, *Literary Criticism in Antiquity* [2 vols.] and *English Literary Criticism* [3 vols.]. For a history from 1750 to the present, consult R. Wellek, *History of Modern Criticism* [4 vols. published thus far]. For English critical theory in the early nineteenth century, consult M. H. Abrams, *The Mirror and the Lamp*. On new criticism, in addition to Brooks's articles cited above, consult M. Krieger, *The New Apologists for Poetry*.)

cuts. Transitions in a film. Within a °sequence (group of related °shots), the transitions are normally made by **straight cuts** – a strip of film is spliced to another, resulting in an instantaneous transfer from one scene to the next. Two older and now rather unfashionable sorts of transition are sometimes still employed, usually between sequences rather than within a sequence. These are the **dissolve** (the scene dissolves while a new scene appears to emerge from beneath it, there being a moment when we get a blur of both scenes), and the **fade** (in the **fade-out** the screen grows darker until black, in the **fade-in** the screen grows lighter until the new scene is fully visible). In effect the camera is saying "Let us now leave X and turn to Y," or "Two weeks later." In *2001* a prehistoric ape-like creature discovers that he can use a bone as a tool, and he destroys a skeleton with it. Then he throws the bone triumphantly into the air, where it dissolves into a spaceship of the year 2001. The point is that the spaceship is the latest of man's weapons and progress is linked with destructiveness. Two older methods, even less in favor today than the dissolve and the fade but used in many excellent old films and in some modern films that seek an archaic effect, are the **iris** (the new scene first appears in the center of the previous scene and then expands until it fills the screen) and the **wipe** (a sort of windshield wiper crosses the screen, wiping off the first scene and revealing the next).

"Cutting" refers to the process of assembling shots into a coherent film; **montage,** a closely related word (from the French *monter,* "to mount"), refers to the completed assemblage. Eisenstein used montage to refer especially to juxtaposed shots of different material which did not further the narrative but which meaningfully brought together different areas of experience, rather as a simile does. Scenes in Eisenstein's *Strike* juxtapose the slaughter of a bull with the shooting of workers. (Consult R. Stephenson and J. R. Debrix, *The Cinema as Art;* and L. R. Bobker, *Elements of Film.*)

dactyl (adjective: **dactylic**). See °versification.

Dadaism. In 1916 the painter Hans Arp (also known as Jean Arp) and some friends chose the infantile term *dada* to signify – they said – everything and nothing. (Some Dadaists said that the word suggested the masculinity that they desired in art, as opposed to the femininity or *mama* that characterized the art they rejected.) In the next few years the emphasis was put on the nothingness: reason and religion, among other things, were regarded as bankrupt, and in an effort to banish clichés poems were made by linking words at random, thus annihilating sense as well as clichés. The movement was succeeded by °surrealism. (Consult *The Dada Painters and Poets, An Anthology,* ed. R. Motherwell; and M. A. Caws, *The Poetry of Dada and Sur-realism.*)

dead metaphor. See °figurative language.

débat. A medieval literary form wherein two speakers (*e.g.*, body vs. soul, owl vs. nightingale) dispute a topic, such as evil or poetry. The form, though it may owe something to the °conventional theme of pastoral contests between singing shepherds, is chiefly indebted to the debates in medieval schools. Somewhat related is the **flyting,** an impromptu folk contest wherein two contenders heap abuse on each other. It occasionally appears in literature, as in the dispute between Beowulf and Unferth in the Old English °epic, *Beowulf*.

decadence. See °Aesthetic Movement.

decorum. See °style.

deism. See °Enlightenment.

denotation. See °connotation.

dénouement. See °plot.

deus ex machina. Literally, a god out of a machine. (1) In Greek drama a god who descends by a crane-like arrangement and solves a problem in the story, thus allowing the play to end. (2) Any unexpected and improbable device (*e.g.*, an unexpected inheritance from a long-lost uncle in Australia) used to unknot a problem and thus conclude the work.

dialogue. (1) A literary work in the form of a conversation, as Plato's *Dialogues*, which are allegedly records of Socrates's conversations on philosophic problems. (2) The speech exchanged between characters, or, very loosely, even the thoughts of a single character, in any literary work. **Stichomythia** is a special form of dialogue, wherein two speakers in a verbal duel alternate speeches of a single line. Example (from *Hamlet*):

> *Queen.* Hamlet, thou hast thy father much offended.
> *Hamlet.* Mother, you have my father much offended.
> *Queen.* Come, come, you answer with an idle tongue.
> *Hamlet.* Go, go, you question with a wicked tongue.

diction. Choice of words, wording. Some poets and critics have felt that only certain words or grammatical arrangements of words are suitable for poetry, and these constitute **poetic diction.** Dr. Johnson, in the eighteenth century, characterized poetic diction as "a system of words . . . refined from the grossness of domestic use"; he objected to the "knife" ("an instrument used by butchers and cooks") which Lady Macbeth says she will use to murder the King. "Words too familiar, or too remote," Johnson said, "defeat the purpose of a poet." Presumably, he would have preferred "blade" or "steel." Similarly, in some poetry shepherds are always "swains," and their sheep are their "fleecy care" or "fleecy wealth." (See °periphrasis.) It should be noted, however, that although the neoclassicists (see °classic) considered some words unsuited by their °connotations for certain lofty kinds of poetry (such as °tragedy and °epic), they used them in forms they thought were lower, such as °satire. That is, words were not so much regarded as unpoetic but rather as suited only for certain kinds of poetry. Speaking broadly, the °romantics (see under °classic) in the late eighteenth and early nineteenth centuries broadened the language of serious poetry by broadening the subject-matter deemed serious. Some of the subjects regarded by the neoclassicists as unsuited for serious poetry (*e.g.*, peasants) were not so regarded by the romantics, who thereby extended the vocabulary of serious poetry.

Diction usually includes word order; thus, the diction of "I saw him" differs from the diction of "Him I saw." Most critics and poets today feel that no words or grammatical constructions are consistently unsuited for literature, but in a particular context all except the right word or construction are unsuited (see °decorum, under °style). An **archaism** – an obsolete word, such as "methinks" – is not inherently poetic or unpoetic, but suitable in some contexts and not in others. T. S. Eliot says (in *On Poetry and Poets*) that every period has its own correct poetic diction, language close to, but not identical with, current speech. (Consult G. Tillotson, *Essays in Criticism and Research*.)

didactic literature. Literature that is explicitly instructive. Here are some didactic lines by John Gay, telling the angler how to clean worms:

Cleanse them from filth, to give a tempting gloss,
Cherish the sully'd reptile race with moss;
Amid the verdant bed they twine, they toil,
And from their bodies wipe their native soil.

Dr. Johnson said that "the task of an author is, either to teach what is not known, or to recommend known truths by his manner of adorning them." Didactic poetry is sometimes opposed to **pure poetry**, which allegedly is devoid of instruction and moral content, and aims not to educate but merely to delight one's aesthetic sensibility by its music or by the pictures it evokes. (Consult G. Moore's *Anthology of Pure Poetry*. For various uses of the term "pure poetry," consult F. A. Pottle, *The Idiom of Poetry*, Ch. V; and R. P. Warren, "Pure and Impure Poetry," *The Kenyon Review*, 5 [Spring 1943], reprinted in *Critiques and Essays in Criticism*, ed. R. W. Stallman.) Vergil's *Georgics*, which tells how to farm, Ovid's *Art of Love*, which tells how to seduce, Pope's "Essay on Man," which tells what man is and what his proper behavior is, are obviously didactic. The term need not be pejorative, though critics who favor "pure poetry" often use "didactic" as a term of opprobrium. It can be argued that all or almost all of the world's great literature is partly didactic: °satire castigates certain kinds of behavior; Milton announced that he wrote *Paradise Lost* in order "to justify the ways of God to men"; and even so simple and direct a °lyric as Shakespeare's "Who is Sylvia?" didactically concludes that because she is "holy, fair, and wise" she deserves our song of praise. The problem, then, is one of degree: didactic literature deals largely and explicitly with instruction. It is not intrinsically any less poetic because of its subject-matter than lines about a rose fluttering in the breeze are intrinsically more poetic because of their subject-matter.

dimeter. See °versification.

Dionysian. See °Apollonian.

director. The coordinator of author, actors, designers, and technicians. Such early directors of film as De Mille and Griffith selected the script, hired the actors, and were concerned with all aspects of making a motion picture. But in the 1930's and 1940's directors tended to come in after the script department had already prepared a script, and they generally completed their job before the editing department edited the film. They were, in short, employees of such studio heads as Samuel Goldwyn. After World War II, however, important directors (*e.g.*, Bergman and Fellini) enlarged their roles, selecting the story and controlling all subsequent work on the film. Such activity produced the ***auteur* theory** – the idea that the "author" of a film is the strong director who imposes his vision on actors, camera men, etc., and who finally produces a film that embodies his vision. (Consult A. Sarris's preface to his *Interviews with Film Directors*, and especially the interviews with Truffaut and Godard.)

dirge. See °elegy.

disclosure (or **discovery**). See °plot and °tragedy.

dissociation of sensibility. In "The Metaphysical Poets" (in *Selected Essays*) T. S. Eliot wrote that for a poet of the late sixteenth and early seventeenth centuries, "a thought . . . was an experience; it modified his sensibility." Such a poet had a unified sensibility, a fusion of intellect and feeling (or perhaps a union of thought and sensation – Eliot is a little vague) which was "constantly amalgamating disparate experience." But "in the seventeenth century a dissociation of sensibility set in." Later poets either thought or felt, but (Eliot says) unlike earlier poets they did not "feel their thought as immediately as the odor of a rose," and the result is inferior poetry wherein, for example, a °metaphor (see under °figurative language) is not essential but is a tacked-on illustration. Eliot returned to the idea in "Milton II" (in *On Poetry and Poets*), stating that "we must seek the causes of this dissociation in Europe, not in England alone." Persons interested in the idea have usually blamed the dissociation on the triumph of scientific rationalism in the later seventeenth century, after which, it is held, poets thought rather than felt, until the romantic reaction (see °classic), when poets felt rather than thought. (Eliot's idea is sharply analyzed in F. Kermode, *The Romantic Image;* by F. W. Bateson in *Essays in Criticism,* 1 [1951], 302–12; and by Bateson and E. Thompson in *Essays in Criticism,* 2 [1952], 207–14.)

dissolve. See °cuts.

distance. See °psychical distance.

dithyramb. An emotional choral °hymn in honor of °Dionysus (see °Apollonian), Greek god of vegetation and wine. From the dithyramb, it is thought, Greek °tragedy developed. More generally, a dithyramb is any wild or emotional song or piece of writing, such as Dryden's "Alexander's Feast." (See °ode.)

documentary. A nonfictional motion picture, usually filming the real — on the spot, not in a studio — in a way that supposedly manifests not only its surface but its inner reality and that makes a social and/or artistic comment. In John Grierson's words, the making of "realist documentary, with its streets and cities and slums and markets and exchanges and factories . . . requires . . . a very laborious, deep-sensing, deep-sympathizing creative effort." Of Robert Flaherty's *Nanook of the North,* Grierson wrote: "*Nanook* was the simple story of an Eskimo family and its fight for food, but in its approach to the whole question of film making was something entirely novel at the time it was made. It was a record of everyday life so selective in its detail and sequence, so intimate in its 'shots,' and so appreciative of the nuances of common feeling, that it was a drama in many ways more telling than anything that had come out of the manufactured sets of Hollywood." (Consult J. Grierson, *Grierson on Documentary,* rptd. in part in *Film, A Montage of Theories,* ed. R. D. MacCann; and R. Manvell, *Film.*) ***Cinéma vérité,*** or "direct cinema," a kind of documentary, uses a hand-held camera to record – rather jerkily – without any premeditated plan, spontaneous happenings such as the goings-on at a party or children playing in the street. Generally this highly mobile camera seeks to catch what Jonas Mekas calls "the free flight of life" (*Film Culture*, no. 21 [Summer 1960], p. 15).

doggerel. See °versification.

domestic drama. See °bourgeois drama and °tragedy.

drama. A presentation wherein actors imitate for spectators a deed ("drama" is derived from Greek *dran*, "to do") by gestures and/or words. The ***mise en scène*** is the staging of the drama, including scenery and **properties** (movable furniture) as well as the positions and gestures of the actors. If the story is communicated entirely through gestures, it is a **pantomime** or **dumb show**, but the latter is often a silent play within a play, as in *Hamlet*, III.ii, where players wordlessly enact the murder of a king.

The two chief dramatic divisions, °tragedy and °comedy, are separately discussed; here follow some of the other types. The **miracle play**, a medieval dramatization of a Biblical story (*e.g.*, Cain and Abel) or of a saint's life, was chiefly popular from the twelfth through the fifteenth centuries. The term is sometimes limited to plays on saints' lives, and Biblical plays are then called **mystery plays.** The plays, especially in the late Middle Ages, included much secular material; *The Second Shepherds' Play*, to take a notable example, devotes six-sevenths of its space to a comedy about a sheep-stealer and one-seventh to the news of Christ's birth. The **morality play**, a later medieval development which remained popular well into the sixteenth century, was an °allegorical dramatization of the conflict between good and evil, including such characters as Everyman, Good Deeds, and Avarice. (Consult A. C. Cawley, ed., *Everyman and Medieval Miracle Plays*; A. Williams, *The Drama of Medieval England*; E. K. Chambers, *The Mediaeval Stage*; and K. Holzknecht, *The Backgrounds of Shakespeare's Plays*. For the morality play and its influence, especially on *Othello*, consult B. Spivack, *Shakespeare's Allegory of Evil*.) The **masque** (or **mask**) was a largely musical entertainment (apparently derived from an ancient °ritual) in the °Renaissance court, wherein aristocrats performed a dignified playlet, usually °allegorical and °mythological, and usually celebrating some aspect of the supernatural power that moves through the actions of kings and noblemen. The masque was lavishly produced, but its basic structure commonly was simple: the masquers (costumed and masked noble performers) enter, supposedly having come from afar; they invite the ladies of the court to dance, they dance, and the masquers depart. In the movement from surprise or uncertainty (caused by the entrance of the costumed masquers) to the celebration of the life-giving force of the monarch or other powerful person in whose honor the masque was held, there is an implication of fertility, or at least of a united society.

Shakespeare's *Henry VIII*, I.iv, dramatizes the masque at which in fact the king met his second wife, Anne Boleyn, but Renaissance England's greatest writer of masques was Ben Jonson, who collaborated with the architect Inigo Jones. Jonson popularized what he called the **anti-masque** (a grotesque dance of monsters or clowns), performed by professionals representing chaos, who are dispelled by the courtly performers. "Anti," from "antic," meaning "a grotesque caper" or "a fool," is sometimes written "ante" because the anti-masque normally precedes the masque. (Consult A. Nicoll, *Stuart Masques and the Renaissance Stage.*)

A **melodrama** was originally a drama with occasional songs, or with music (*melos* is Greek for "song") expressing a character's thoughts, much as it does in films today. By the early nineteenth century such plays had become so stereotyped that the word acquired a second (and now dominant) meaning: a drama wherein characters clearly virtuous or vicious are pitted against each other in sensational situations filled with °suspense. The situations, not the characters, are the chief source of interest. The element of exotic horror (castles with dungeons) dominant in early nineteenth-century melodramas was often replaced later in the century by local horror (the cruel landlord), but whether exotic or local, melodrama is improbable, and virtue triumphs over unlikely circumstances. In short, hostile critics of melodrama argue that it falsifies human character, presenting heroes and villains, and falsifies life, presenting events that move toward unhappiness but then – with little internal logic – end happily. In contrast to tragedy, the conflict in melodrama is external – between hero and villain, rather than within the hero himself, who in a tragedy is struggling for self-knowledge – and the outcome is an unambiguous triumph over external evil – rather than the tragic hero's attainment of self-knowledge. (Consult R. B. Heilman, *Tragedy and Melodrama;* and F. Rahill, *The World of Melodrama.*)

A relatively recent dramatic °genre is the **problem play.** Though one can argue that any drama poses a problem (In a °tragedy, are the gods just? In a °comedy, ought a father to interfere with his son's marriage?), a problem play invites attention to a sociological problem of some sort. Ibsen's *A Doll's House* invites debate on the relation between husband and wife; Shaw's *Major Barbara* similarly invites debate on the merit of the Salvation Army, the ethics of industrialists, and the responsibility for war. A problem play may or may not be tragic or comic, but the emphasis is on the social problem rather than on the destiny of particular characters.

If a drama is suited only for reading and not for acting, it is a **closet drama.** Most poetic nineteenth-century dramas (*e.g.*, Shelley's, Coleridge's, Browning's) fit into this category, though Byron's plays have recently been moving out of the closet. (For the structure of drama, see °plot and °irony; for the chief types, see °comedy and °tragedy. Consult A. Nicoll, *World Drama;* A. R. Thompson, *The Anatomy of Drama* [2nd ed.]; E. Drew, *Discovering Drama*; and R. Peacock, *The Art of Drama.*)

dramatic illusion. The notion that the reader or spectator voluntarily enters into the world of the piece of literature, suspending (as Coleridge says in *Biographia Literaria,* Ch. 22) "denial and affirmation." This state, between delusion (the spectator thinks the world on the stage is real) and full awareness (the spectator never forgets he is looking at scenery and actors), Coleridge characterizes (Ch. 14) as "that willing suspension of disbelief for the moment, which constitutes poetic faith." See °psychical distance.

dramatic monologue. In some degree almost every poem can be called a dramatic monologue: a single speaker is saying something to someone, even if only to himself. Frost's °lyric beginning "Whose woods these are I think I know" is an obvious example. But whereas the speaker of a lyric usually seems to be the poet, the speaker of a dramatic monologue is a fictional character (*e.g.*, a duke who has eliminated his last duchess) or a historical figure (*e.g.*, Fra Lippo Lippi) caught at a critical moment, not so much expressing an emotion and singing as undergoing an experience while talking. His utterance is conditioned by the situation, and is usually directed to a silent audience (*e.g.*, an emissary to the duke). The speaker commonly reveals aspects of his personality of which he himself is unaware; in "My Last Duchess," Browning's duke is insufferable but doesn't know it. T. S. Eliot's "The Love Song of J. Alfred Prufrock," wherein the speaker's timid self addresses his aggressively amorous self, is a variant of the form. (Consult R. Langbaum, *The Poetry of Experience.*)

dream vision. A literary form wherein the author records his alleged dream. Such dreams are usually °allegorical, frequently presenting an ideal world. In Bunyan's *The Pilgrim's Progress*, the narrator dreams of a man named Christian who journeys to the Celestial

City. In the Middle Ages, the dream vision was often highly °conventional: in May the sleepless poet is reading a book; he dozes and dreams that he is guided by a deity or person or beast into a place (often a garden) where various allegorical events occur; and when the poet awakens he invites the reader to interpret the dream. Chaucer's *The Book of the Duchess* is a notable example of this kind. Literature no less than life abounds in dreams. In *Alice's Adventures in Wonderland*, Alice dreams about a world inside a rabbit hole; in Joyce's *Finnegans Wake*, H. C. Earwicker dreams – it is difficult to say about what – for more than 600 pages.

dubbing. The process of adding sound (words, music, sound effects) to a film. The sound tracks of foreign films are often replaced by sound tracks in English. In °documentary films, a narrative track is often added, explaining the visual images (a sweating Malaysian is seen in a grove of rubber trees, and a cool British voice says, "The rubber is tapped from trees . . .").

dumb show. See °drama.

eclogue. See °pastoral.

edition. (1) All the copies of a work printed from a single setting of type. (2) A work with relevant comment (*e.g.*, an introduction or notes), such as H. E. Rollins's edition of Keats's letters, which seeks to present an accurate text (not an easy task, considering Keats's deletions, abbreviations, etc.) and to elucidate obscure points.

Einfühlung. See °empathy.

elegiac quatrain. See °versification.

elegy. In Greek and Latin verse, a poem in alternate lines of dactylic hexameters and dactylic pentameters (see °versification). Much Latin love poetry was in this meter, but so too were **eulogies,** poems praising the living or the dead, rather like Ben Jonson's "To the Memory of . . . William Shakespeare." In the modern languages, until Gray wrote his "Elegy Written in a Country Churchyard" in the middle of the eighteenth century, an elegy was any gentle poem written in pairs of rhyming lines. Gray's "Elegy," however, is in stanzas of four lines, and its enormous popularity helped to limit "elegy" to a melancholy or mournfully contemplative poem or a poem of lament. Especially if the elegy is a short funeral lament, it may be called a **dirge,** which in ancient times was a funeral song. A **threnody** and a **monody** are also funeral poems, though the monody is often longer and more complex. The elegy of lament is frequently a °pastoral, wherein shepherds mourn the death of a fellow shepherd. If a reader does not understand the value of °conventions (traditional themes or subjects) in literature, he may find such a lament – with its usual °invocation (see °figurative language) to the Muses, its procession of mourners, and its list of flowers – frigid. But that the conventions provide a good poet with a meaningful and familiar °ritual which he can fill to great advantage can be seen in elegies as diverse as Milton's "Lycidas" and Whitman's "When Lilacs Last in the Dooryard Bloomed." (Consult T. P. Harrison and H. J. Leon, *The Pastoral Elegy*.)

elision. The omission of part of a word, as in "o'er" ("over"), or "th'earth" ("the earth").

Elizabethan. Of or pertaining to the reign of Queen Elizabeth I (reigned 1558–1603) of England. (See °Renaissance.)

emblem book. A book with drawings (emblems) whose significances are interpreted in moral °allegory by accompanying prose or verse. The verse (**emblematic poetry**) interpreting the picture in an emblem book is sometimes an image itself, *i.e.*, in the shape of a cross, an altar, wings, etc. (See °shaped poetry. Consult R. Freeman, *English Emblem Books*.)

emotive meaning. See °connotation.

empathy. The projection of one's feelings into a perceived object. It is what the Germans call ***Einfühlung*** – "a feeling into." Vernon Lee, one of the formulators of the idea, claimed that when we say "the mountain rises" we do so not because the mountain in fact rises (it doesn't) but because we have often raised our eyes, head, and total muscular structure to look at mountains or other tall objects. In perceiving a mountain, we merge (unawares) its image with the previously accumulated idea of rising. It is a sort of °personification (see °figurative language), wherein man feels himself into something not himself. The doctrine (which has been much disputed) is sometimes simplified and equated with **sympathy,** the identification with a perceived object wherein the perceiver trembles along with a leaf which actually is trembling, or is terrified along with a terrorstruck person whom he perceives. Wordsworth, in *The Prelude*, says that

> my favorite grove
> Tossing in sunshine its dark boughs aloft
> Wakes in me agitations like its own.

(Consult V. Lee's essay in *A Modern Book of Esthetics*, ed. M. Rader; and H. S. Langfeld, *The Aesthetic Attitude*, partly reprinted in E. Vivas and M. Krieger, *The Problems of Aesthetics*.)

encomium. A laudatory speech or poem, glorifying (for example) a person, a place, or an abstraction. (See °ode.)

end-rhyme. See °versification.

end-stopped line. See °versification.

enjambment. See °versification.

Enlightenment. Broadly, the eighteenth century; more specifically, the intellectual movement during the eighteenth century which held (to state the matter in its most extreme form) that man need not wait for God's grace to perfect him in heaven, but can attain perfection on earth by distrusting special divine revelations and dogma, and by trusting reason and scientific experiment (the "logic of facts"). Not all neoclassical writers (see °classic), of course, held so extreme a view, but the great degree to which rationalism and empiricism penetrated the thought even of a Roman Catholic can be seen in these lines from Alexander Pope's "Essay on Man":

> Say, first, of God above, or man below,
> What can we reason but from what we know?
> Of man, what see we but his station here,
> From which to reason, or to which refer?
> Through worlds unnumbered though the God be known,
> 'Tis ours to trace him only in our own.

Pope goes on to censure man's pride in reason, but he nevertheless urges man to see – by reason – that he is to submit to God's plan. The prevailing religion of the Enlightenment was **deism,** a belief that (1) a benevolent rational deity created the universe; (2) the universe is therefore operated according to fixed rules; (3) the deity reveals Himself not through any special scriptures (such as the Bible) to a chosen few but rather reveals Himself to all men's reason; (4) He should be worshipped; and (5) the best form of worship is moral behavior. Such a belief outlawed miracles and sects, regarding them as narrow-minded superstitions that conflicted with reason. Again we can quote Pope, who, though doubtless a sincere Catholic, is strongly colored by the deism which in fact conflicts with Catholicism:

> For modes of faith let graceless zealots fight;
> His can't be wrong whose life is in the right.

There is a hint of Christian thinking in the pun on "graceless," but Pope's suggestion that matters of belief are unimportant would not go unchallenged by Catholics (or by most Protestants) today. Deists usually subscribed to the idea that all creation was a great **Chain of Being,** which ranged from God down through the heavenly hierarchy to man, and then continued down through animals and plants to the lowest sort of inert matter. What to man seems to be evil has its place in this chain, and without this apparent evil the world would be inferior. God in his goodness created every possible thing (the principle of plenitude), and the elimination of, say, earthquakes, would from the divine point of view produce an inferior universe. Thus, this is the best of all possible worlds – a conception Pope presented superbly in his *Essay on Man,* and Voltaire ridiculed superbly in his *Candide.* (Consult E. Cassirer, *The Philosophy of the Enlightenment;* A. O. Lovejoy, *The Great Chain of Being;* and B. Willey, *The Eighteenth-Century Background.*)

envoy (or **envoi**). (1) A concluding stanza of a poem, dedicating the poem, commonly to a prince. (2) A poem of farewell.

epic. A long serious poem telling a story about a hero and his heroic companions, often set in a past that is imagined as greater than the present. The hero often has superhuman or divine traits; in Homer's *Iliad* the hero (Achilles) is the son of a goddess; in Milton's *Paradise Lost* the characters are God the Father, Christ, angels, and Adam and Eve. The action is usually simple (*e.g.*, the wrath of Achilles, the fall of man), but it is amplified by °allusions and °figurative language that give it cosmic significance. The style is appropriately elevated to the greatness of the deeds (Milton's poem "with no middle flight intends to soar / Above the Aonian mount, while it pursues / Things unattempted yet in prose or rhyme"), and certain °conventions (*i.e.*, traditional procedures) are usually observed. For example, the poet conventionally appeals to the Muses for aid, asking them what started the °action (the **epic question**), and he often begins his narrative in the middle of things (***in medias res***), with the hero at his lowest fortune (*e.g.*, the *Iliad* begins with the Greeks in despair), and later tells the earlier portions of the story. Commonly, too, there is an epic catalog, or list, as of ships in the *Iliad* and fallen angels in *Paradise Lost*. Gods (called the **machinery**) often participate in the story, helping the heroes, and there is frequently a trip to the underworld. The **epic simile** (or **Homeric simile**) is an extended comparison (see °figurative language) wherein a subject is compared to something that is presented at such length or in such detail that the subject is momentarily lost sight of. In *Paradise Lost*, Satan walking in Eden is compared to a vulture.

> Here walk'd the Fiend at large in spacious field.
> As when a Vultur on Imaus bred,
> Whose snowy ridge the roving Tartar bounds,
> Dislodging from a Region scarce of prey
> To gorge the flesh of Lambs or yeanling Kids
> On Hills where Flocks are fed, flies toward the Springs
> Of Ganges or Hydaspes, Indian streams;
> But in his way lights on the barren Plains
> Of Sericana, where Chineses drive
> With Sails and Wind their cany Waggons light:
> So on this windy Sea of Land, the Fiend
> Walk'd up and down alone bent on his prey.

The epic is sometimes divided into two species: the **primary epic** (occasionally called a "primitive epic" or a "folk epic") is a stately narrative about the nobility and recited to the nobility; the **secondary epic** (occasionally called a "literary epic" or an "artificial epic") is a stately narrative about great events, designed not for a courtly assembly who hears it recited but for a literate man who reads it in a book. Examples of the primary epic are Homer's *Iliad* and *Odyssey*, and the anonymous Old English *Beowulf*; examples of the secondary epic are Vergil's *Aeneid* and Milton's *Paradise Lost*. The poet of the primary epic is a °bard who speaks impersonally as the voice of the community, whereas the poet of the secondary epic commonly has more individuality; Homer is not introspective, Milton sometimes is. Homer's poems and *Beowulf* (as opposed to the *Aeneid* and *Paradise Lost*) have in common that they are products of a "heroic age" (*i.e.*, an age when virtue is largely identified with courage and strength, and when poets sing of these virtues). Because the poets in heroic societies composed the poem while they sang about traditional episodes, their lines abound in **stock °epithets** (*e.g.*, Homer's recurrent "rosy-fingered dawn") and repeated lines. Such repetitions, especially if they repeatedly occur at a particular position in the line, are called **formulas;** they not only afforded pleasure to the hearers by their familiarity but also helped the poet compose. An oral poet, that is, composed by drawing upon his stock of traditional stories and °motifs or °*topoi* (*e.g.*, the royal banquet, the descent to the underworld) and his stock of traditional formulas (*e.g.*, Agamemnon is "king of men"). An obvious imitation of this formulaic poetry is Longfellow's *The Song of Hiawatha*. (On formulas, consult A. B. Lord, *The Singer of Tales;* and W. Whallon, *Formula, Character, and Context*. For the descendants of the epic, see °novel. Consult C. S. Lewis, A

Preface to Paradise Lost; E. M. W. Tillyard, *The English Epic and Its Background;* and, for the importance of the oral tradition, C. Whitman, *Homer and the Heroic Tradition,* Ch. VI; and R. Scholes and R. Kellogg, *The Nature of Narrative,* Ch. 2.)

epigram. Originally "an inscription," for the Greeks it became a short poem, usually solemn, and almost never stinging. Walter Savage Landor's "On His Seventy-fifth Birthday" is an imitation:

I strove with none: for none was worth my strife,
  Nature I loved, and next to Nature, Art;
I warmed both hands before the fire of life,
  It sinks, and I am ready to depart.

But with the Romans, especially with Martial, the word came to mean a short witty poem, barbed at the end. Here is an example by John Wilmot, Earl of Rochester:

We have a pretty witty King,
Whose word no man relies on,
Who never said a foolish thing,
Nor ever did a wise one.

The word has also come to mean any cleverly expressed thought, whether in verse or prose. King Charles II's reply to Rochester is an example: he said his words were his own, his acts were those of his ministers. (Consult M. Hodgart, *Satire,* pp. 158–63.)

epilogue. (1) An appendix (usually a concluding address) to a composition; or (2) the actor who recites such an appendix to a play (*e.g.,* Rosalind, at the close of *As You Like It*).

epiphany. Literally, a "showing-forth," especially of a deity. James Joyce first made the word current in literary criticism. A person may make a gesture – say, a sudden movement of the hand – which shows his state of mind. An epiphany is such a sudden revelation of the inner essence or "whatness" of an object, character, situation, or experience, usually manifested by physical details. In his later works Joyce used complex suggestions of words to express the "sudden manifestation" of experience. In *Finnegans Wake* Earwicker's fall is epiphanized by the exclamation "O Foenix culprit," which combines (among other things) foe, *felix culpa* (Latin for "happy fault"), the Phoenix Park Murders, and phoenix-bird. (Consult I. Hendry, "Joyce's Epiphanies," in *James Joyce,* ed. S. Givens; W. T. Noon, *Joyee and Aquinas;* and F. L. Walzl, *PMLA,* 82 [1967], 152–4.)

episode. (1) In Greek tragedy, the portion between two choral °odes. (2) In a °plot, a portion having some unity of its own, an incident. A work of **episodic structure** consists of units or episodes loosely connected but coherent in themselves (*e.g.*, an adventure story consisting of one hunt after the other), rather than of a single complete unit from which nothing can be removed without doing great violence to the whole. (See °form and °novel.)

epistle. A letter. The "verse epistle," such as Pope's "Epistle to Dr. Arbuthnot," is a poem couched in the form of a letter. The **epistolary °novel** is a long prose fictitious narrative consisting chiefly or entirely of letters, such as Samuel Richardson's *Pamela* or J. P. Marquand's *The Late George Apley.*

epitaph. A burial inscription, often serious but sometimes humorous. The following example is John Gay's own epitaph:

> Life is a jest and all things show it;
> I thought so once, but now I know it.

epithalamion (or **epithalamium**). A °lyric poem, usually joyous and ceremonial, in honor of a bride or bridegroom or both. The poem is not simply in praise of marriage, but of a particular marriage. The ancient Greeks publicly recited such pieces, but those written by the Roman Catullus were most influential in England and France. Spenser's "Epithalamion" (the greatest in English) begins, like one of Catullus's, with an °invocation and follows Catullus in calling on young people to attend the bride, in describing the ritual cry, "Hymen io Hymen," in praising the bride, and in welcoming the night. To the Catullan material Spenser adds deep Christian feeling and realistic descriptions of Irish landscape. (For details consult T. M. Greene, "Spenser and the Epithalamic Convention," *Comparative Literature,* 9 [1957], 215–28.)

epithet. A word or phrase expressing a characteristic of someone or something, such as "*lily-livered* coward," or "William *the Conqueror.*" A **stock epithet** is one used repeatedly, such as Homer's "fleet-footed Achilles" or "ox-eyed Hera." (See °epic and °periphrasis. For °transferred epithet, see °figurative language. On eighteenth-century epithets, see G. Tillotson, *Augustan Poetic Diction.*)

epode. See °ode.

epyllion. See °idyll.

Erziehungsroman. See °novel.

escape literature. Writing designed to allow the reader to forget the cares of this life while he enters a never-never land, or outer space.

Peter Pan, Twenty Thousand Leagues under the Sea, The Rustling at Cattle Creek, and most "true romances" are examples. Such writing presumably gratifies readers' fantasies, and thus may serve a useful purpose. Charles Lamb said that after reading certain works which were totally unrelated to the world as he knew it: "I come back to my cage and my restraint the fresher and more healthy for it."

essay. A composition having no pretension to completeness or thoroughness of treatment. The word comes from the French *essai* (an attempt), first applied in 1580 by Montaigne to his short writings, but the form is ancient. Though usually prose, an essay may be in verse (*e.g.*, Pope's "Essay on Criticism"). Because the chief implication in the word is "a tentative study," essays often comprise only a few pages (Bacon's and Montaigne's are sometimes less than a page), but there is no fixed length. There have been books of essays, and even large books containing a single essay, but since the eighteenth century, essays have appeared chiefly in periodicals. Notable contributors include (among many) Addison, Steele, Lamb, Hazlitt, Macaulay, George Orwell, and Aldous Huxley. The eighteenth-century essay was usually short and didactic, enlivened with anecdotes and sketches of characters; essentially it told its reader how a cultivated man should live. The °romantic writers (see under °classic) around 1800 especially cultivated the **informal** or **familiar essay;** in the familiar essay, such as Lamb's "Dissertation upon Roast Pig," the author is chatty and personal, often revealing as much about himself as his subject. **Formal essays,** such as Locke's *Essay Concerning the Human Understanding,* are impersonal analyses. (Consult L. Fiedler's annotated anthology, *The Art of the Essay;* and H. Walker, *The English Essay and Essayists.*)

establishing shot. See °shot.

eulogy. See °elegy.

euphemism. A mild or vague word or phrase replacing one considered offensively direct. Example: "comfort station." See °periphrasis.

euphony. Pleasant combination of sounds. Presumably, the ear is pleased by Tennyson's "Round and round the spicy downs the yellow Lotos-dust is blown." Of the consonant sounds, *l, m, n, r, y,* and *w* are often regarded as the most euphonious. An unpleasant combination of sounds is **cacophony.** The cacophony in Matthew Arnold's lines in praise of Shakespeare, "And thou, who didst the stars and sunbeams know, / Self-school'd, self-scann'd, self-honor'd, self-secure, / Didst tread on Earth unguess'd at," is presumably unintentional (certainly it is unfunctional in the poem and a defect). But the cacophony in E. E. Cummings's "the glush of / squirting taps plus slush of foam knocked off" suits the total poetic effect. (For sound effects, see °versification, especially °onomatopoeia.)

euphuistic. See °style.

exegesis. See °explication.

exemplum. A °parable (see under °allegory) or moralizing tale, especially in a medieval sermon. In Chaucer's "Pardoner's Tale," the passage narrating the death of "riotoures thre," is the exemplum in a sermon on greed.

existentialism. A philosophical theory which has gained considerable renown, especially in Europe since World War II. Its stress upon the °subjective as central has facilitated its adoption as a point of view for words of literature. The philosophical and literary writings of existentialists (especially Jean-Paul Sartre) stress the insecurity, loneliness, and irrevocability of man's experience; the perilous situations in which these characteristics are most salient; and the serious, involved, and anxious striving of responsible men to face these situations, or the evasive, desperate, ultimately futile attempts of weak men to escape them. Most existentialists think that the future is undetermined and that man is free. But man also has neither fixed potentialities nor fixed values to guide him. We make our own characters and assert our own values as valid, in our free choice of actions. In Sartre's terminology, "existence precedes essence" and "man makes himself"; that is, man has existence before he has any defined character, and he must himself form his character. Existentialist criticism examines literature by asking how well it portrays these complexities of man's situation. (Consult J.-P. Sartre, *What is Literature?*; and W. Barrett, *Irrational Man*.)

explication (or **exegesis**). A "close reading" of a literary text. The term derives from the French secondary school's method – *explication de texte,* wherein the meaning is unfolded from words. To point out a °pun (see under °figurative language), that is, to unfold two or more meanings from one word, is an act of explication; to point out a plagiarism is not. Explication focuses on the meaning of a literary work; *The Explicator,* a journal devoted to the method, announces that "material concerned with genesis, parallelism, or biography cannot . . . be accepted unless it has a direct bearing upon the interpretation of the text." (See also, under °criticism, °new criticism.) A warning: Robert Frost said,

"Poetry is implication. Let implication be implication. Don't try to turn implication into explication."

exposition. See °plot.

expressionism. A movement dominant especially in German painting during the decade following World War I. The expressionist presents in his work not life as it appears on the surface to the dispassionate eye, but rather life as he (or as his character) passionately feels it to be. Thus his work consciously distorts the external appearance of the object in order to represent the object as it is felt. Scenery in an expressionist °drama will not be photographically accurate but will be distorted so that, for example, the wall in a courtroom may veer crazily to reflect the defendant's state of mind. Among the classics of expressionism are O'Neill's *The Hairy Ape* and the film, *The Cabinet of Dr. Caligari.* (See M. Gorelik, *New Theaters for Old.*)

fable. (1) A brief tale, in verse or prose, making little or no pretense to being historical; because it is often derived from °folklore, it frequently has a child-like quality. Sometimes a moral is tacked onto such a tale, but a fable differs from a °parable (see under °allegory) in that the moral of a parable is diffused throughout the story. The characters are often animals who speak and act like human beings, as in Aesop's *Fables.* (Consult *Aesop's Fables,* trans. D. B. Hull.) (2) Sometimes used synonymously with °plot.

fabliau. An earthy, humorous medieval tale in verse or prose, usually °satirizing the clergy and middle-class life, and often obscene. The stock situation is a triangle of jealous husband, lecherous wife, and crafty clerk. An example is Chaucer's "Miller's Tale." (Consult C. Muscatine, *Chaucer and the French Tradition.*)

fade-in, fade-out. See °cuts.

falling action. See °plot.

falling meter. See °versification.

farce. See °comedy.

fast film. See °film.

feminine ending. See °versification.

fiction. Anything made up or imagined, especially a prose narrative. (See °novel, °short story, and °literature.)

figurative language. Robert Frost said, "Poetry provides the one permissible way of saying one thing and meaning another." This, of course, is an exaggeration, but it shrewdly suggests the importance of figurative language – saying one thing in terms of something else. Words have their literal meaning, but they can also be used so that something other than the literal meaning is implied. A girl is a girl, but a doll, a peach, or, as Damon Runyon would have it, a mouse can also be a girl. What is literally impossible may, through figures of speech (also called **tropes**), be highly interesting, significant, and moving. "My love is a rose" is literally nonsense, for she is not a five-petalled, many-stamened plant with a spiney stem. But the suggestions of "rose" include "delicate beauty," "soft," "perfumed," and thus the word "rose" can be meaningfully applied – figuratively, rather than literally – to "my love."

When a reader comes upon "Caesar growled," he is forced (if the context has indicated that Caesar is a man) to take "growled" in a nonliteral way. Understanding that Caesar did not literally emit the sound of, say, a lion or a bear, he takes the word's suggestions (°connotations). Here the figure stands for (approximately) "Caesar's menacing talk showed irritation, unreason, feelings beneath a man." Why does a writer bring a menagerie into a description of Caesar? Because by this indirect way he can most vividly and most accurately describe Caesar. Consider how, by indirectly speaking of the beloved, Burns richly gives us a strong impression of her and of his feeling toward her: "O my luve's like the melodie / That's sweetly played in tune." The terms **tenor** and **vehicle** are often used in discussing figurative language. The tenor is the gist of the thought concerning the subject (Caesar's personality, or the girl's loveliness), and the vehicle is that which embodies the tenor – the analogy (*e.g.*, the animal in the case of Caesar, music in the case of the girl) by which the tenor is conveyed. Notice, however, that although figurative language usually moves in the direction of concreteness (jealousy is a "green-eyed monster"), it need not: "He is ignorance itself." There is abundant terminology for nonliteral language. The following are the most common figures.

A **simile** is an explicit comparison between essentially unlike things, introduced by a connective (*e.g.*, "like," "as," "than") or a verb such as "seems":

My heart is like a singing bird. (C. Rossetti)

I wandered lonely as a cloud. (Wordsworth)

I am weaker than a woman's tear. (Shakespeare)

Seems he a dove? His feathers are but borrowed. (Shakespeare)

(For the epic simile, see °epic.) If the speaker omits "like," "as," or "than," making, say, the literally impossible assertion "My heart is a singing bird," he uses a **metaphor.** Just as "Caesar growled" contains terms that are literally incompatible, so "My heart is a singing bird," by its incompatible terms (impossible terms, we might say), forces the hearer to regard the connotations rather than the denotation of one term. If we do not have both terms ("My winged heart" instead of "My heart is a bird"), we have an implicit or **submerged metaphor.** In Milton's "all these and more came flocking," if "all" referred to sheep, "flocking" would be literal; but because "all" refers to pagan deities, "flocking" is metaphoric, implicitly replacing, approximately, "in a crowd like a group of sheep." A **mixed metaphor** combines two metaphors, often ludicrously: "Let's iron out the bottlenecks." Dr. Johnson was so bothered by the mixture in Macbeth's "My way of life / Is fall'n into the sear, the yellow leaf," that he suggested "way" was a misprint for "May"; few other readers find the mixture disturbing. A **dead metaphor** has lost its figurative value: the *eye* of a needle, the *foot* of a hill.

In **metonymy** the name of one thing is used for another which it suggests or is closely related to. For example, if a letter is said to be in Milton's "hand," it means that the letter is in Milton's own handwriting. When Lyndon Johnson and John Kennedy were competing for the Democratic nomination for the presidency, Johnson said that the office needs a man with a little gray in his hair, *i.e.*, age and wisdom. In **synecdoche** a part of something is substituted for the whole, or the whole is used in place of one of its parts. "Ten sail" thus stands for ten ships; "bread" in "give us this day our daily bread" stands for food in general. A **transferred epithet** is a word or phrase shifted from a noun it would normally modify to one in the neighborhood, as in Gray's "drowsy tinklings," where "drowsy" literally modifies the sheep who wear the bells, but is here figuratively applied to the bells. In present usage the distinction between these figures is so slight that the word "metonymy" covers synecdoche and all transferred epithets.

The attribution of human characteristics or feelings to nonhuman organisms, inanimate objects, or abstract ideas is **personification** or **prosopopoeia.** Examples are: Tennyson's "Now sleeps the crimson petal, now the white," and Shakespeare's reference to "Time's cruel hand." (Consult M. Bloomfield in *Modern Philology,* 60 [1962–63], 161–71, reprinted in his *Essays and Explorations.*) John Ruskin, in *Modern Painters* (1856), called the attribution of human feelings to inanimate things the **pathetic fallacy.** Thus, to speak of "the cruel crawling foam" is to employ the pathetic fallacy, for the ocean is not cruel (glad to inflict pain), although it may seem so to men who suffer from it. Ruskin disapproved of such misstatement, allowing it only in poetry where the speaker is so moved by passion that he cannot be expected to speak more accurately. But in great poetry, Ruskin held, the intellect is not thus conquered. The term, however, is now often used without this pejorative implication. Often closely related to personification is the **apostrophe,** in which a thing is addressed directly, as though it were a listening person. Apostrophe and personification go together in Donne's "Busy old fool, unruly Sun," and in Wyatt's "My lute, awake." In Milton's apostrophe, "Yet once more, O ye laurels," there is personification only in the faint hint that the laurels are listening creatures. An apostrophe may be addressed to a person (in which case, of course, there is no personification) if the person is not to be conceived of as literally listening, as in Wordsworth's "Milton! thou should'st be living at this hour." If the address is to a deity whose aid is sought (as is common at the beginning of an °epic), it is an **invocation,** such as Milton's "Sing, Heavenly Muse," at the beginning of *Paradise Lost*.

Exaggeration is **hyperbole** or **overstatement,** as in Prince Hal's characterization of Falstaff as "this horse-breaker, this huge hill of flesh." The opposite of exaggeration is **understatement,** an assertion that states less than it indirectly suggests, as in Swift's "Last week I saw a woman flayed, and you will hardly believe how much it altered her person for the worse." A special form of understatement, **litotes,** affirms something by negating its opposite. Thus: "He's no fool" means "he is shrewd." (See, under °irony, °verbal irony.) The °epigrammatic combination of contradictory or incongruous terms is **oxymoron:** "living death," "mute cry," or Milton's description of hell as "No light, but rather darkness visible." "Sense transfer," or **synesthesia,** is a description of one sensory experience in terms of another; Emily Dickinson speaks of a fly's "blue, uncertain stumbling buzz," and we all speak of "loud colors."

A **pun** (or **paronomasia**) involves words similar or identical in sound, suggesting two or more meanings simultaneously in a word or phrase. In *Romeo and Juliet*, as Mercutio dies he says: "Ask for me tomorrow, and you shall find me a *grave* man." (The Greek term "paronomasia" is sometimes limited to words near but not identical in sound, *e.g.*, "hear" : "hair," but not "hair" : "hare.") Related to the pun is the **portmanteau word,** Lewis Carroll's term for a word coined by combining two words and which (Carroll's Humpty Dumpty says) contains "two meanings packed up into one word." Examples are "slithy" (slimy and lithe) and "chortle" (chuckle and snort). Allied to the pun is William Empson's use of **ambiguity.** Ordinarily, an ambiguous statement is one with two or more incompatible meanings. For example, the Delphic oracle prophesied that if Croesus waged war on Cyrus, he would destroy a great empire; encouraged, Croesus went to war, but the oracle was ambiguous, and the empire he destroyed was his own. Ambiguity is thus, in most discourse, undesirable. But in poetry we need not always choose between meanings; if poetry, as Ezra Pound says in "How to Read" (*Literary Essays*), is more "highly charged" than prose, though doubt about what is meant may be undesirable, multiple meanings may be desirable and relevant. Empson, in *Seven Types of Ambiguity*, seized on a nonpejorative sense of the word, defining ambiguity as "any verbal nuance, however slight, which gives room for alternative reactions to the same piece of language." He thus uses the word in the sense of "an expression with several relevant suggestions." The word "assassination" in *Macbeth* reminds Empson of "hissing." He attempts to discriminate between enriching ambiguities (involving "intricacy, delicacy, or compression of thought") and worthless ones (due to "weakness or thinness of thought").

(For other important figures see °allegory, °irony, °paradox, °symbol, and, under °metaphysical poets, °conceit. Among the most penetrating discussions of figurative language, especially of metaphor, are M. C. Beardsley, *Aesthetics*; and I. Hungerland, *Poetic Discourse*.)

figure (figura). See °type.

film. Fast film is highly sensitive and requires less light to catch an image than **slow film** does, but it is usually grainier. Perhaps because newsreels commonly use fast film a grainy quality is often associated with realism. Moreover, because fast film shows less subtle gradations from black to white than slow film does, its harshness makes it especially suitable for *The Battle of Algiers* but unsuitable for musical comedies or romantic subjects.

fin de siècle. See °Aesthetic Movement.

flashback. See °plot.

flyting. See °*débat*.

foil. See °plot.

folio. (1) A large sheet of paper, folded once to form two leaves (four pages). (2) A book consisting of sheets folded once, providing four pages each (such as the first collected edition of Shakespeare's plays, published in 1623). If the sheets are folded twice, each supplying four leaves and eight pages, the book is a **quarto.** If folded three times, an **octavo.** (3) More commonly today, these terms are applied to the page-size rather than to the construction of a book. An Elizabethan folio, then, is large – almost the size of *Life* magazine; a quarto is about seven inches by nine inches; an octavo is about five inches by seven inches.

folklore. The general term given to songs, tales, sayings, and (though here we go beyond literary folklore) dances and customs such as initiation rites, practical jokes, and holiday celebrations, which are passed down from generation to generation, usually orally. "Folklore" seems to have been coined in 1846; before that, such materials were called "popular antiquities." Among **folksongs** are °ballads, worksongs, children's counting-out rhymes, and nursery rhymes. The **folk tale** includes semi-historical accounts (*e.g.*, °anecdotes about Lincoln), legends connected with historical persons (*e.g.*, George Washington and the cherry tree, and tall tales of Davy Crockett), thoroughly fanciful accounts of supernatural creatures (stories of Paul Bunyan, of witches, and of talking animals). The original authorship of folk literature is usually unknown, but even if a piece (such as "Casey Jones," or the tale about Washington's cherry tree) has been traced to a single author, it is folklore if the common people have adopted it and transmitted it among themselves. (Consult *A Treasury of American Folklore*, ed. B. A. Botkin; R. Dorson, *American Folklore;* and Stith Thompson's massive *Motif-Index of Folk Literature.*)

A **folk play,** such as the one Thomas Hardy describes in *The Return of the Native,* is a play of unknown authorship, probably derived from an ancient °ritual which has been passed down and performed by people as a traditional activity. (Consult E. K. Chambers, *The English Folk-Play,* which studies plays of death and resurrection.) Recently in America, however, "folk play" has been applied to simple plays which, stressing pageantry and local tradition, are put on by amateurs in towns celebrating historical events such as the arrival of the *Mayflower.*

foot. See °versification.

foreshadowing. See °suspense.

form. Commonly, a literary kind, type, or °genre. °Drama is one form, the °novel another; or the form of drama can be subdivided into such forms as °comedy, °tragedy, °melodrama, etc. Nondramatic poetry can be subdivided into such forms as °epic, °elegy, and °*débat;* or the forms can be distinguished on the basis of °meter and °rhyme scheme: the sonnet, the limerick, and the quatrain (see °versification) are forms. In another sense, form is equated with **structure,** or overall design or arrangement of material. For example, Lincoln's Gettysburg Address involves a movement from the remote past ("four score and seven years ago") to the recent past (the war) to the present (dedication of the cemetery). The arrangement of °episodes in a °novel can be said to make up the form (or structure) of the novel; if there is no ordering principle, the episodes being like so many coins tossed onto a table, the work can be said to have no structure (see °plot). Similarly, a sonnet (see °versification) which organizes its argument by moving from the general to the particular (it is spring and all creatures are joyful; why am I sad?) has a different form from one which moves from particular to general. This last sort of form is easily discerned in Shakespeare's "Sonnet 73":

> That time of year thou may'st in me behold
> When yellow leaves, or none, or few, do hang
> Upon those boughs which shake against the cold,
> Bare ruined choirs where late the sweet birds sang.
> In me thou see'st the twilight of such day
> As after sunset fadeth in the west,
> Which by-and-by black night doth take away,
> Death's second self, that seals up all in rest.
> In me thou see'st the glowing of such fire
> That on the ashes of his youth doth lie,
> As the deathbed whereon it must expire,
> Consumed with that which it was nourished by.
> This thou perceiv'st, which makes thy love more strong
> To love that well which thou must leave ere long.

In the first twelve lines there is a **parallel** (repeated) **structure:** the speaker in four lines compares his age to autumn, then in four more lines to twilight, then in four more lines to a dying fire. In the final two lines he comments on the attitude of a friend who has perceived his state. This poem moves by parallels; another poem might be built on **antithesis,** moving from one proposition to a statement of its opposite. Here is a single line from Hamlet:

> With mirth in funeral, and with dirge in marriage.

The syntax is parallel, but there are antitheses between "mirth" and "funeral," and between "dirge" and "marriage." (Consult R. Wellek and A. Warren, *Theory of Literature*, Ch. 16.)

When we get down to arrangements within a line, however, we are examining what some critics call **texture** rather than structure. John Crowe Ransom, in *The New Criticism*, contrasts structure (what some people would call the bare bones, the prose paraphrase) with **texture** (°imagery, °meter, °concrete details, etc.). Both structure and texture within themselves often have **tension;** that is, there is a state of strained relations between, say, general and particular, or between the rhythm of speech and the rhythm of a poem, or between the poem's rhyme and the thought that threatens to overflow it. Textural details play against other textural details, just as the larger structural units play against (by paralleling, say) other units. For some critics, tension gives form. Heraclitus, a Greek philosopher of the late sixth century B.C., said: "As with the bow and the lyre, so with the world: it is the tension of opposing forces that makes the structure one." (See °unity.)

It can be argued that the concepts of structure and texture are misleading if they are thought of as something apart from **content.** Structure, for example, assumes that the writer has some content, and proceeds to parcel it out into lumps of one sort (*e.g.*, parallels) or another (*e.g.*, contrasts). But the very *arrangement* of the content may change the content. Take so simple a statement as the title of a Soviet film, "Great Is My Country." Had a different arrangement been used ("My Country Is Great"), the content would have been different, for the Soviet title contains not a mere statement about Russia but also, by virtue of its inversion, the speaker's view that Russia is so great that normal word order is inadequate. "Great Is My Country" is probably closer to "My country is unimaginably wonderful, and I'm terribly proud of it," than it is to "My country is great." The point is that while the division between form and content may hold true of some writing ("Place an egg in boiling water" is the same, in a cookbook, as "Into boiling water put one egg"), literature makes so subtle a use of language that alterations in form (arrangement, organization) often cause alterations in content (the thing arranged). Take Donne's lines to his beloved, " 'Twere profanation of our joys, / To tell the laity our love." Those who look on °style as a garment of thought will hold that Donne's lines are a dressed-up way of saying "It degrades our pleasures to tell the uninitiated of our passion." But those who feel that form and content are inseparable believe that this **paraphrase** (rewording) loses an important part of the meaning, for, they argue, Donne's "profanation" and "laity" imply that his love is holy, and the paraphrase loses this essential meaning. Even if one holds that an elaborate paraphrase can capture most or perhaps all that the poem asserts, obviously the paraphrase loses much of the poem that is valuable – *e.g.*, memorable brevity and patterns of sound. (See °style. Consult *Style in Prose Fiction*, ed. H. C. Martin.)

formula. See °epic.

fourteener. See °versification.

frame (or **still**). A single photograph in a motion picture. Normal projection speed is twenty-four frames per second.

frame story. A narrative within which are other narratives, such as Boccaccio's *Decameron,* where the "frame" (a group of people leave Florence in plague-time) allows for the inclusion of other narratives (the tales the exiles tell each other). Other examples are *The Arabian Nights* or Chaucer's *Canterbury Tales.*

free verse. See °versification.

general and **particular.** See °concrete.

genre. A literary species or °form, *e.g.,* °tragedy. (Consult R. Wellek and A. Warren, *Theory of Literature;* and E. D. Hirsch, *Validity of Interpretation,* Ch. 3.)

Georgian. Pertaining to the reign of any king named George, but "Georgian poetry" is commonly the poetry written during the reign of George V of England (reigned 1910–36). Sir Edward Marsh, who popularized the phrase "Georgian poetry" by editing several anthologies with that title between 1911 and 1920, excluded most of the best writers of these years (*e.g.,* Hardy, Yeats, Eliot) and included writers (*e.g.,* John Masefield) who, broadly speaking, seem to deal pleasantly and decoratively but rather casually with nonurgent themes. The poets, often chatty, frequently write about serene country life; when we recall that they lived during World War I, they seem to look backward.

georgic. See °pastoral.

gloss. An explanation, short or long. Coleridge himself provided marginal glosses to his *The Rime of the Ancient Mariner.*

gnomic poetry. See °aphorism.

Golden Age. In ancient Greek thought (the term was coined by Hesiod in the eighth century B.C.), the first and best period, an age when Kronos or Saturn ruled the world, and men lived a simple life without discord or labor, the earth yielding abundant fruits in a perpetual springtime. This lost world was followed by a Silver Age, when man became impious, and then by a Bronze Age, when militant men destroyed each other. The last and worst age is the present, the Iron Age, when men are violent and dishonorable.

By extension, the Golden Age is the best period of any sort of history; thus the Renaissance can be said to be the Golden

Age of English drama, and Augustan Rome the Golden Age of Roman literature.

Arcadia, a relatively isolated region in Greece, was celebrated in Roman literature (by Ovid and Vergil) as an idyllic pastoral place, where men lived as in the Golden Age. But in Ovid and Vergil there is a note of sorrow at the contrast between Arcadian happiness and the suffering visited upon men elsewhere. Sannazaro's loose narrative, *Arcadia* (1504), goes further, mingling sorrowful songs with celebrations of an ideal rural life. The idyllic concept of Arcadia was diminished still further by the phrase "*Et in Arcadia ego*" (Latin: "I am present even in Arcadia") which first occurs in the early seventeenth century, spoken by Death. Often mistranslated as "I too have been in Arcadia," *i.e.*, "I once was happy," the phrase gave a still deeper melancholy to the idea of Arcadia. The pastoral image of happiness, however, continued tenuously, though by the beginning of the present century W. B. Yeats could say "The woods of Arcady are dead." The Golden Age, regularly set in a lost past, is a complement to °Utopia, which looks to the future. (See °pastoral and °primitivism. Consult H. Levin, *The Myth of the Golden Age in the Renaissance*.)

Goliardic verse. Latin lyrics named for one Golias, a poet to whom some are ascribed. They are mostly by medieval wandering scholars, are frequently off-color, and commonly praise a carefree life of wine and women. (Consult G. F. Whicher, *The Goliard Poets*.)

Gothic. When used pejoratively, the term means "crudely medieval," "lacking °classical order," or "barbaric." But the term has also been employed by those (*e.g.*, John Ruskin) for whom lack of classical order is a virtue, hence it can mean "delightfully varied," "exuberant." The **Gothic Revival,** in the later eighteenth century, was an elegant toying with the delightful melancholy evoked by moss-covered ruins, decaying old churches, and crumbling gravestones (see °Graveyard School). This sense of "Gothic" (*i.e.*, "interestingly gloomy," "mysterious," "morbidly attractive") is at the root of the **Gothic novel,** a long prose narrative of horror, often involving eerie medieval castles with secret passageways, ghosts, and a virgin harried by a villain who himself is tortured by mysterious guilt. Horace Walpole's *Castle of Otranto, a Gothic Story* (1764) was the first of a line which has stressed horror; William Faulkner's *Absalom, Absalom!* is not the last. Notable Gothic novels written between these are Matthew Lewis's *The Monk* and Mary Shelley's *Frankenstein;* Dickens's *Great Expecta-*

tions, with Miss Havisham's cobwebbed and rat-infested chamber, also belongs in part to this tradition. (Consult K. Clark, *The Gothic Revival* [2nd ed.]; and G. Sherburn, "The Restoration and Eighteenth Century," in *A Literary History of England,* ed. A. C. Baugh.)

Graveyard School. Eighteenth-century poets who wrote melancholy poems on death. The most notable product of the school is Thomas Gray's "Elegy Written in a Country Churchyard." Graveyard poems are part of the °Gothic Revival of the eighteenth century, but they go back to Milton's "Il Penseroso" with its "drowsy charm," its "high lonely tower," and its

> . . . storied windows richly dight,
> Casting a dim religious light.

Greek romance. See °novel.

hagiography. See °biography.

hamartia. See °tragedy.

heptameter. See °versification.

heroic couplet. See °versification.

heroic drama. See °tragedy.

heroic quatrain. See °versification.

hexameter. See °versification.

high angle shot. See °shot.

Homeric simile. See °epic.

hovering stress. See °versification.

hubris. See °tragedy.

Hudibrastic verse. See °versification.

humanism. See °Renaissance.

humor, humor character, comedy of humors. See °comedy for all three.

hybris. See °tragedy.

hymn. A song in praise of God or any holy creation, or of gods or heroes, usually to be sung by a chorus. The word has occasionally been used for poems on lofty topics: *e.g.,* Spenser's "Hymn in

Honor of Love" and Shelley's "Hymn to Intellectual Beauty." (See °ode.)

hyperbole. See °figurative language.

hypermeter. See °versification.

iamb (adjective: **iambic**). See °versification.

idyll. A short picturesque piece, usually a poem about shepherds (a °pastoral), but sometimes applied to what some critics call the ***epyllion,*** a little °epic. The *epyllion* presents an episode from the heroic past, but it stresses the pictorial and romantic rather than the heroic. The chief English example is Tennyson's *Idylls of the King,* with its elaborate depiction of several Arthurian episodes. W. Allen, Jr., in *Studies in Philology,* 55 (1958), 515–18, argues that the term *epyllion* is useless.

imagery. Now usually defined as the sensory content of a literary work. A few decades ago it was commonly held that images evoked pictures (Wordsworth's "host of golden daffodils"), and it was sometimes held that images were not literal but were produced by °figurative language ("My heart is like a singing bird"). But today it is agreed that images involve any sensations (including those of heat and pressure as well as those of eye, ear, etc.), and that the literal sensory objects in the work (the heart as well as the singing bird to which it is compared) are images. In Keats's "Ode to a Nightingale," the bird whom he addresses is an image, so is the incense of the flowers (not visible, but olfactory), and so too is the dryad to which the bird is figuratively compared. In Wordsworth's poem, the daffodils themselves are images, so too is the breeze (which is normally felt rather than seen), and so too are the dancers to whom the daffodils are figuratively compared. However, no image is in the phrase, "Hope is perpetual." Alexander Pope's "Hope springs eternal in the human breast" has an image not only in "the human breast" but also (very faintly) in "springs," for "springs" suggests something that is material and in motion. (Consult N. Friedman, "Imagery: From Sensation to Symbol," *Journal of Aesthetics and Art Criticism,* 12 [1953], 25–37; P. N. Furbank, *Reflections on the Word "Image"*; and I. Hungerland, *Poetic Discourse.*)

Imagists. A group of poets, chiefly American, of whom the most notable are Ezra Pound and Amy Lowell. Influenced by T. E. Hulme's insistence on precise and complex images, Imagists (at their height, 1912–14) sought to use common speech, to regard all the world as possible subject-matter, and to present a sharply perceived detail in a concentrated concrete visual image. They usually wrote °free verse (see °versification); the classical example of Imagist poetry is Pound's "In a Station of the Metro":

> The apparition of these faces in the crowd;
> Petals on a wet, black bough.

(Consult G. Hough, *Image and Experience*.)

imitation (Greek: ***mimesis***). (1) Not a pejorative term in much criticism, for it often implies a "re-creating" or "re-presenting" of a form in a substance not natural to it. Michelangelo imitated the form of Moses, in stone. For Aristotle °tragedy is the imitation (re-presentation, re-creation), through words, gesture, music, and scenery, of an important action. (2) A piece of literature that loosely copies another piece of literature, a sort of free translation, with the allusions of the original replaced by allusions more appropriate to those of the language of the translation. Alexander Pope published *Imitations of Horace,* which ranged from translations of Horace to passages that are Horatian merely in tone. In our time, Robert Lowell has published a volume called *Imitations.*

in medias res. See °epic.

incremental repetition. See °ballad.

intentional fallacy. The alleged error of interpreting a work according to the author's intention. Such a procedure is said to be fallacious because we rarely know the author's intention. Even when he states his intention, it may not correspond to his accomplishment. Thomas Mann said he wrote *Buddenbrooks* "as a lark," but it need not be judged on that basis. (Consult W. K. Wimsatt, Jr., *The Verbal Icon;* and M. C. Beardsley, *Aesthetics.*)

intercut. See °sequence.

interior monologue. See °novel.

invective. See °satire.

inversion. A reversal of normal order. A notorious example is Browning's "Irks care the crop-full bird? Frets doubt the maw-crammed beast?" which, of course, means "Does care irk . . . , does doubt fret . . . ?"

invocation. See °figurative language and °epic.

iris. See °cuts.

Irish bull. See °bull.

irony. Socratic irony is named for Socrates, who commonly feigned more ignorance than he possessed, presenting himself as ignorant when he was in fact cautious or tentative. The man who plays the understater ("I do not understand; please explain to me . . .") is a Socratic ironist, and his words are ironic.

In **verbal irony** there is a contrast between what is stated and what is more or less wryly suggested. As Robert Frost puts it, "In irony, the tone indicated contradicts the words." Thus Pope attacks the proud man by ironically encouraging his pride:

> Go, wiser thou! and, in thy scale of sense,
> Weigh thy opinion against Providence. . . .
> Snatch from His hand the balance of the rod,
> Re-judge His justice, be the God of God.

What is stated ironically need not be the reverse of what is suggested; irony may, for example, state somewhat less than it suggests, as in this °understatement: "Men have died from time to time." Verbal irony that is crude and heavy-handed rather than clever is commonly called **sarcasm.**

In addition to ironic treatment there is ironic content, commonly called by any of three names: **dramatic irony,** or **Sophoclean irony,** or **tragic irony.** Here "irony" refers to a condition of affairs that is the tragic reverse of what the participants think. The spectators understand the speech or action more fully than do the dramatic figures. Thus it is ironic that Eve eats the forbidden fruit; she expects great happiness, but it brings great sorrow. Macbeth kills Duncan, thinking he will then achieve happiness; he later finds he loses all that makes life worth living. Sophocles's King Oedipus accuses the blind prophet of corruption, but by the end of the play Oedipus learns (as the audience knew at the outset) that he himself is corrupt, that he has been mentally blind (ignorant) and that the prophet has had vision (knowledge). Oedipus meant what he said, but his words prove to be ironic. Similarly, the words of the high priest on Jesus' execution, "It is expedient for us that one man should die for the people," meant one thing to the priest but mean something else for Christians, who see that Jesus died "for the people" in a larger sense. As in verbal irony, there is here an element of contrast; the contrast, however, is not between what the speaker says and what he means, but between what he says or thinks and the true state of affairs. This sort of irony, based on misunderstanding or partial knowledge, is common in tragedy, but comedy too has its misunderstandings, and "irony" (though of course not "tragic irony" or "Sophoclean irony") is used to describe comic speeches wherein the speaker's words contrast (unknown to him) with the facts or deeds that bring about results opposite to those he anticipates.

More generally, the contrast implied in "irony" need be neither tragic nor comic; it is "ironic" that the strong man is overthrown by the weak man and that the liar unknowingly tells the truth. When slightly simple-minded Gulliver praises the ingenuity with which his countrymen destroy themselves in warfare, though Gulliver's praise is sincere, Swift's is ironic.

Irony of fate (a phrase which H. W. Fowler's *Modern English Usage* aptly says is hackneyed), or **cosmic irony,** denotes the view that God, or fate, or some sort of supernatural figure, is amused to manipulate human beings as a puppeteer manipulates his puppets. Thus, by an irony of fate the messenger delivers the prisoner's pardon an instant too late.

Romantic irony is more common in German (especially of the late eighteenth and early nineteenth centuries) than in any other literature. The romantic ironist detaches himself from his own artistic creation, treating it playfully or objectively, thus presumably showing his complete freedom. He may set forth noble ideals, and then declare that science has proved them mere illusions. Byron's Don Juan, on shipboard, bids a tender farewell to Spain and to his beloved, vows to think only of her, and suddenly grows seasick. The use of contradictory elements or moods within the work thus allies romantic irony to the modern critical use of the term °paradox, for both sometimes imply that the artist aims to grasp the world's contradictory totality.

I. A. Richards uses "irony" to denote "the bringing in of the opposite, the complementary impulses," and suggests (in *The Principles of Literary Criticism*) that irony in this sense is a characteristic of poetry of "the highest order." R. P. Warren, explaining the importance of the bawdy Mercutio in *Romeo and Juliet,* says (in *The Kenyon Review,* Spring 1943) that "the poet wishes to indicate that his vision has been earned, that it can survive reference to the complexities and contradictions of experience. And irony is one such device of reference." In this sense, irony is synonymous with one meaning of °**wit** (for a history of the word, see °comedy). That is, "wit" sometimes refers to the presence of material within a literary work that apparently contradicts other parts of the work and thus supposedly induces a balance. Whereas I. A. Richards and R. P. Warren speak of irony as "the bringing in of the opposite" and the "reference to the complexities and contradictions of experience," T. S. Eliot in his *Selected Essays* says that "wit" in Andrew Marvell's poetry provides an "internal equilibrium" by its "recognition . . . of other kinds of experience which are possible." (Consult G. G. Sedgewick, *Of Irony;* A. R. Thompson, *The Dry Mock;* A. E. Dyson, *The Crazy Fabric: Essays in Irony;* and D. C. Muecke, *The Compass of Irony.*)

Jacobean. Of or pertaining to the reign of James I (Latin: Jacobus) of England (reigned 1603–25). The word often connotes "disillusion," an alleged quality of the period. But this view, which looks chiefly at writers like Donne, Webster, and Tourneur, is too simple, for it neglects many masterpieces, notably Bacon's *Advancement of Learning,* the King James version of the Bible, and Shakespeare's *The Tempest.* (Consult U. Ellis-Fermor, *The Jacobean Drama;* and D. Bush, *English Literature in the Earlier Seventeenth Century.*)

kenning. See °periphrasis.

Künstlerroman. See °novel.

lai (or **lay**). A song, or, more commonly, a short fanciful medieval tale of love and/or adventure.

lampoon. See °satire.

leitmotif. See °motif.

light verse. Playful poetry. Older light verse is generally highly polished and in elaborate stanzaic forms (see °versification). It often combines light-heartedness or whimsy with a mildly °satiric thrust, as in Suckling's "Why So Pale and Wan, Fond Lover?" which concludes: "If of herself she will not love, / Nothing can make her: / The devil take her." But since the late nineteenth century, light verse has often included less elegant pieces, such as nursery songs, with humorous rhymes and distorted pronunciations. The **limerick** is a jingling poem of three long and two short lines, the long lines (first, second, and fifth) rhyming with each other, the short lines (third and fourth) rhyming with each other. The rhyming words after the first line are sometimes misspelled, producing a humorous effect:

> Once a Frenchman who'd promptly said "oui"
> To some ladies who'd asked him if houi
>   Cared to drink, threw a fit
>   Upon finding that it
> Was a tipple no stronger than toui.

The **clerihew** is a kind of light verse named for its inventor, Edmund Clerihew Bentley. It names a person and includes an alleged bit of biography. Example:

> Sir Christopher Wren
> Said, "I am going to dine with some men.
> If anybody calls
> Say I'm designing St. Paul's."

Nonsense verse makes absurd assertions. It often jingles and uses nonexistent words, thus combining pleasant orderly sounds with absurdities which frustrate the intellect. Lewis Carroll's "Jabberwocky" begins, " 'Twas brillig, and the slithy toves, / Did gyre and gimble in the wabe." ***Vers de société*** is light verse of the older sort – genial, graceful, sophisticated °lyric poetry, often with a complicated rhyme-scheme, lacking both the sharp satire and the unsophisticated humor of much other light verse. (Consult *The Silver Treasury of Light Verse*, ed. O. Williams; and *The Oxford Book of Light Verse*, ed. W. H. Auden. N. Douglas and G. Legman have compiled anthologies of bawdy limericks.)

limerick. See °light verse.

literature. Sometimes means anything written, as in "Please send me literature on breeding guppies." Most critics regard such a definition as too broad because it includes pamphlets on how to make money from guppies, and too narrow because it excludes such oral compositions as °ballads and °folk tales. Perhaps one can begin by saying that literature uses language in compositions that are valuable in themselves. A pamphlet on breeding guppies is valuable chiefly as a guide to breeding guppies; a °short story about a man who breeds guppies is valuable (if it has value) chiefly in itself. Furthermore, this story – or poem or play – is recognized as a fiction; it is not historical, but imaginative, and the reader finds this fictitious man and his world interesting. The story may begin by claiming to be historical, and it may be set in a real city (Dublin) during a recognizable era (early twentieth century); but it is nevertheless accepted by the reader as a fiction, just as the spectator at a play accepts the scene in front of him as a fiction, although it too is set in Dublin. There is, in short, an element of make-believe. The poet may say (as Tennyson says in *In Memoriam*), "Dark house, by which once more I stand." Perhaps Tennyson did stand by the house as he wrote the lines, but probably he didn't. In any case, though he seems to address the house, the reader, not the house, is in fact listening.

In addition to this element of make-believe, there is in literature (as opposed to other compositions of words) considerable importance in the arrangements of sound and in the richness of suggestion. In fact, richness of suggestion is often said to distinguish **poetry** from **verse.** True, poetry and verse are sometimes equated: any metrical composition (*i.e.*, a composition with stresses at more or less regular intervals) can be called "poetry" or "verse." But a distinction is often made between verse and poetry: verse is metrical discourse, but poetry is verse wherein, in addition to there being an element of make-believe, the sounds and the °connotations (suggestions, related associations) play an important part. Thus, "Thirty days hath September, / April, June, and November" is verse but not poetry, for the sounds (aside from the metrical pattern that makes the words easily remembered) are not of much importance, and the words do not suggest more than they explicitly say. Because poetry (as opposed to verse) is suggestive, it usually employs °figurative language:

O, my luve's like a red, red rose,
  That's newly sprung in June.

Robert Burns packs into the comparison between a woman and a rose suggestions of such things as delicacy, fragrance, and the texture and color of a woman's cheeks.

Another use of the word "poetry" is important, and this brings us back to the idea that literature involves a sort of sophisticated make-believe. For Aristotle, "poetry" is more or less what we would call "fiction." In this view, an artistic composition – whether metrical or not – is poetry, as opposed to history, for it is not totally subservient to mere fact. Poetry defined as imaginative creation would include, for example, *Gulliver's Travels, A Tale of Two Cities*, and Plato's myths. This view of poetry as fiction, as a harmonious patterned representation, rather than as meter, has the advantage of suggesting – what is surely true – that a novel and a narrative poem have more in common than a novel and a textbook (though both the latter are prose) and that "Thirty days hath September" has more in common with a textbook on calendars than it has with a poem by Tennyson. (Consult D. Daiches, *A Study of Literature*.)

litotes. See °figurative language.

local color. See °realism.

long shot. See °shot.

low angle shot. See °shot.

lyric. Originally, a poem to be sung to a lyre; now a short poem (regardless of °meter or of °rhyme scheme), wherein the speaker primarily expresses his emotion or records a meditation, rather than narrates a tale. Lyrics range from Robert Burns's drinking song, "Auld Lang Syne," through Robert Frost's short reflective poems, to George Herbert's religious meditations. Another way of putting it is to say that they range from naming an emotion and singing about it, to undergoing an experience and talking about it. Probably the most common emotion in lyrics is love (or the despair brought on by unrequited love), though grief, pain, etc., also serve. The following is an example of a lyric, from an early sixteenth-century songbook:

Western wind, when wilt thou blow,
  The small rain down can rain?
Christ, if my love were in my arms
  And I in my bed again!

If the emotion is contempt or hate, and it is wittily expressed, the poem is probably better called a °satire or (if brief) an °epigram. A **complaint** is a lyric uttering dissatisfaction, usually to an unresponsive mistress. Chaucer wrote "A Complaint to His Lady" and a humorous "Complaint to His Purse." The latter begins:

To you, my purse, and to noon other wight,
Complayne I, for ye be my lady dere!

During the romantic period (see °classic), nature as well as love became a major subject; the poet (such as Wordsworth) more often expresses his reaction to clouds and daffodils than to his beloved. The **conversation poem** (from Coleridge's "To a Nightingale: A Conversation Poem") was an important lyrical form in the romantic period. Indebted to the later eighteenth-century reflective poem, the conversation poem is characterized by colloquial idiom and by a mixture of description and meditation: usually the poet is led by some stimulus (*e.g.*, the song of a bird) to meditate upon the scene and to transform it, by the power of imagination, from transient phenomena to a higher reality, but normally at the end of the poem he returns to the world of ordinary phenomena. (For longer lyrical forms, see °elegy and, especially, °ode. Consult C. M. Ing, *Elizabethan Lyrics;* H. J. C. Grierson, *Lyrical Poetry from Blake to Hardy;* and C. Brooks, *The Well-Wrought Urn.*)

macaronic verse. Verse containing a mixture of languages, or containing words resembling foreign words. Example:

Mademoiselle got the croix de guerre,
For washing soldiers' underwear,
Hinky-dinky, parley-vous.

machinery. See °epic.

malaprop, malapropism. An unintentionally comic substitution of words. Mrs. Malaprop (*mal* and *à propos*) in Sheridan's *The Rivals* (1775) scatters them profusely. Example: "I would have her instructed in geometry that she might know something of the boundaries of contagious countries."

mannerism. See °style.

Märchen. See °short story.

masculine ending. See °versification.

mask. See °persona and °drama.

masque. See °drama.

maxim. See °aphorism.

meaning. See °connotation and °figurative language.

medium shot. See °shot.

melodrama. See °drama.

memoir. See °biography.

Menippean satire. See °satire.

metaphor. See °figurative language.

metaphysical poets. A group of poets, chief of whom are John Donne (1572–1631) and his seventeenth-century followers, Andrew Marvell, George Herbert, Abraham Cowley, Richard Crashaw, and Henry Vaughan, who reacted against the °conventions (traditions) of °Elizabethan love poetry and wrote a more colloquial, °witty, °ironic, and (in the eyes of some modern critics), at the same time, more passionately intense and more psychologically probing poetry. Instead of writing melodious lines on the lady's beauty (which is like a rose), or even on her indifference (which is like ice), the metaphysicals wrote colloquial and often metrically irregular lines, filled with difficult and unusual metaphors. A far-fetched metaphor or simile is a **conceit;** originally a "concept" or "idea," the "conceit" came to mean a striking ingenious parallel between two highly dissimilar things, such as the comparison of the sun partly obscured by a cloud to a lover whose head is resting on a pillow. Certain **Petrarchan conceits** – named for the Italian sonneteer Petrarch (1304–74) – were much repeated in England. Example: the lover is a ship tossed in a storm, agitated by his own tears, and frozen by the chilliness of his mistress. The **metaphysical conceit** is perhaps not fundamentally different, though sometimes it is more far-fetched and less trivially ornamental, and it is generally more original. The fact that metaphysical conceits were novel rather than traditional, and that they were often drawn from areas not commonly thought of as "pretty" – such as the humble world of commerce, the intellectual world of medieval philosophy, and the esoteric world of chemistry – means that they usually strike the reader with an effect quite different from the Petrarchan conceit. Donne's most famous conceit, in "A Valediction: Forbidding Mourning," compares two lovers to the two legs of a draughtsman's compass; and in "The Ecstasy" he tells his beloved:

> Our hands were firmly cemented
> With a fast balm which thence did spring,
> Our eye-beams twisted, and did thread
> Our eyes upon one double string.

Considerably less successful is John Cleveland's description of a poet writing on the death of a friend:

> I am no poet here; my pen's the spout
> Where the rain-water of my eyes run out.

The term "metaphysical" was applied to Donne by Dryden (Donne "affects the metaphysics"), and extended to the school by Dr. Johnson. It is somewhat misleading, for Donne's poetry, and that of his fellows, is not so much a philosophical account as a psychological exploration of attitudes toward women and God. The metaphysical poet may seem to be philosophic as he advances his hypotheses and definitions (often qualified with "but" and "yet," and concluding with "so"); nevertheless the poem is more concerned with passion than with logic. The impudent and °ironic definitions, for example, often seem °paradoxically to suggest deep feeling. T. S. Eliot sees in their poetry "a direct sensuous apprehension of thought, or a recreation of thought into feeling." Dr. Johnson, who characterized their poetry as presenting the "discovery of occult resemblances in things apparently unlike," was less impressed than Eliot: "The most heterogeneous ideas are yoked by violence together; nature and art are ransacked for illustrations, comparisons, and allusions; their learning instructs, and their subtlety surprises; but the reader commonly thinks his improvement dearly bought, and, though he sometimes admires, is seldom pleased." (Consult D. Bush, *English Literature in the Earlier Seventeenth Century;* J. Bennett, *Five Metaphysical Poets;* E. Miner, *The Metaphysical Mode from Donne to Dryden;* R. M. Adams, *Strains of Discord;* and *The Metaphysical Poets,* ed. H. Gardner.)

meter. See °versification.

metonymy. See °figurative language.

mimesis. See °imitation.

miracle play. See °drama.

mise en scène. See °drama.

mock epic, or **mock heroic.** See °burlesque.

monody. See °elegy.

monologue. See °soliloquy.

monometer. See °versification.

montage. See °cuts.

mood. See °atmosphere.

morality play. See °drama.

motif. A recurrent word, phrase, situation, object, or idea. Most frequently, "motif" is applied to a situation that recurs in various literary works, *e.g.*, the rags-to-riches motif. But a motif (in the following sense sometimes called a **leitmotif,** from the German "leading-motif") can occur within a single work: it is any repetition that helps unify a work by potently recalling its earlier occurrence and all that surrounded it. Examples are the periodic striking of Big Ben in Virginia Woolf's *Mrs. Dalloway* and the ubiquitous discarded circular in James Joyce's *Ulysses*. (See °*carpe diem*, °topic, °*ubi sunt*, and °archetype.)

motivation. See °plot.

mystery play. See °drama.

myth. (1) Sometimes "myth" is synonymous with °plot, denoting the fictional happening (*e.g.*, Oedipus's murder of his father, and his consequent deeds) in a narrative or drama. (2) Mark Schorer (in his *William Blake*), defines "myth" as "a large, controlling image that gives philosophic meaning to the facts of ordinary life. . . . All real convictions involve a mythology. . . . Wars may be described as the clash of mythologies." A myth, then, in the broadest usage is any idea, true or false, to which people subscribe. Thus, one can speak of the "myth" of democracy or of totalitarianism. Because the myths that were sacred truths for pagans were falsehoods for Christians, "myth" sometimes means any imaginary person, place, thing, or idea, such as the myth that the majority is necessarily right. But several other definitions must also be considered. A myth has sometimes been defined as a narrative, usually anonymous, of the origins of life and/or of the deeds (present or future) of supramortal creatures, often explaining the whys and wherefores of natural phenomena. For example, a Zulu myth explains that rain is the tears of the rain-god weeping for a beloved slain bird. A **mythopoeic** mind makes a myth, and a group of myths is a **mythology.** Though these tales are commonly anonymous and traditional, and often evoke deep emotional response and arouse belief, any similar tale made up by an author (such as those in Ovid's *Metamorphoses*) to entertain an unbelieving audience is similarly a myth. Plato's myths are mostly °allegories, frankly invented, with an X = Y relationship. For example, in the "Myth of the Cave" (*Republic*, Book VII), the cave stands for the world of appearances, the sun for the Idea of the Good, etc. "Myth" has also been used to refer to any fictional world, even a highly detailed one that is alleged to be historical. Thus, one can talk about the "myth of England" in Shakespeare's history plays – where English history is seen through the eyes of a playwright.

Myths in the sense of primitive legends about gods, heroes, external nature, etc., have often been regarded by modern men as mere fantasies and legends, or as primitive explanations of natural phenomena, inferior to the explanations supplied by reason and experiment. But in recent years myth has been increasingly dignified, partly because Freud and Jung regarded it as akin to dreams – that is, as a "language" which, properly understood, tells us things otherwise unrevealed. Eric Fromm (see below) says that myths and dreams are "a language in which inner experiences, feelings and thoughts are expressed as if they were sensory experiences, events in the outer world." Perhaps the literary critics most interested in myth are those who assume the existence of °archetypes – unconscious memories of the repeated experiences of the race, such as birth, mating, death. They hold that a myth (like some dreams) is not a mere fanciful creation but the expression of an archetype, revealing hidden attitudes and experiences. It is hard, however, to see how a study of myths is useful in evaluating literature, for good and bad literary works have been written on the same myth. There are numerous dramas on the myth of Oedipus, but surely some are better than others. Perhaps a solution is to say that the artistically superior version moves us more, stirring in us an increased awareness of the depths of life, of our own possibilities and limitations, and thus it reveals a hidden reality. The artistically (effectively) handled myth strikes us as meaningful, even though we cannot rationally explain its meaning, but the poorly handled myth strikes us (it can be said) as meaningless and chaotic. (Consult H. J. Rose, *A Handbook of Greek Mythology*; and R. Graves's controversial two-volume *The Greek Myths*. For the influence of classical myths on English poetry, consult D. Bush, *Mythology and the Renaissance Tradition*, and his *Mythology and the Romantic Tradition*. On myth and mythmaking, consult the Spring 1959 issue of *Daedalus* or the augmented book-version, *Myth and Mythmaking*, ed. H. A.

Murray. For the interpretation of some famous myths, consult E. Fromm, *The Forgotten Language*. On literature and myth, see N. Frye, in *Relations of Literary Study*, ed. J. Thorpe.)

narrative. A story (long or short, prose or poetic, etc.) told by a teller and thus differentiated from a play. (See °plot; for types, see °epic, °short story, °novel.)

narrator. See °point of view.

naturalism. Sometimes defined as the technique of portraying "a scientifically accurate, detached picture of life, including everything and selecting nothing." More commonly, however, it alludes not to a panoramic view or even to the detailed presentation of a narrow **slice of life** (French: ***tranche de vie***), but to a particular attitude held by some writers since the middle of the nineteenth century. Though claiming to be dispassionate observers, they were influenced by evolutionary thought, and regarded man not as possessed of a soul and of free will, but as a creature determined by his heredity and environment. For example, Theodore Dreiser and Frank Norris, who are often indignant at the destructive effect of the factory system on the lives of the workers, present detailed accounts of biologically and/or sociologically predestined characters. Naturalism should not be confused with °realism. (Consult O. Cargill, *Intellectual America*. On naturalistic drama, see *TDR: The Drama Review*, 13, no. 2 [Winter 1968].)

negative capability. John Keats's term, which he cryptically glossed (in a letter of December 21, 1817) as the ability to be "in uncertainties, Mysteries, doubts, without any irritable reaching after fact & reason." Most men, Keats held, lacked this capability; they do not perceive the complexities of reality but, in an effort to clear up all their uncertainties, they rather distort reality by filtering it through their own personality. The great poet, on the other hand, has the ability to escape from or negate his own personality and thus open himself fully to the complex reality around him. Negative capability is sometimes identified with °empathy, sometimes with °objectivity. Keats further discusses the idea (though he does not there use the term) in a letter of October 27, 1818.

neoclassicism. See °classic.

neoplatonism. See °Platonism.

New Comedy. See °comedy.

new criticism. See °criticism.

New Wave (or ***nouvelle vague***). A movement in film around 1960, marked by a highly improvisatory style. The camera is highly mobile, tilting and panning (see °shot) and °zooming, sometimes blurring the image as the camera moves (instead of °cuts) from one speaker to another. The spectator has a strong sense both of the °director's presence and of an unstable, anarchic world of alienated people. Irrelevancies abound. Actual locations – instead of studio sets – are commonly used for interiors as well as exteriors. The movement thus has affinities with °*cinéma vérité* (see under °documentary) and with the °*auteur* theory (see under °director). Examples are Resnais's *Hiroshima, Mon Amour* (1959), and Truffaut's *The 400 Blows* (1959) and his *Jules and Jim* (1961). (Consult *The New Wave*, ed. P. Graham; and *Interviews with Film Directors*, ed. A. Sarris.)

nonsense verse. See °light verse.

nouvelle vague. See °New Wave.

novel and **romance.** A novel is a fictional prose °narrative, of substantial length. No specific required length sets the novel apart from the °short story, and the terms "short novel" or **novelette** or "long story" are sometimes applied to prose fiction that seems too long (say, more than fifty pages) for a short story, yet too short (say, less than one hundred pages) for a novel. Because the novel is a narrative that does not limit itself to historical facts but creates fictional personalities dwelling in an imaginary world (even though this imaginary world may be minutely described as, say, Dublin on June 16, 1904), it is related to the °epic, a long narrative poem. But the epic usually includes gods and men of exceptional or even supernatural ability, whereas the novel, descended partly from °biography, °memoir, and history, usually presents a world close to our own. The title of Fielding's greatest novel – *The History of Tom Jones, a Foundling* – shows some of these characteristics.

We shall return to the novel in a moment, but it may be well here to describe another sort of long narrative fiction, the **romance.** The **Greek romance** may go back to the second century B.C., but most of the extant ones are from the second and third centuries A.D. Indebted to Greek New Comedy (see °comedy), travelers' tales, and the °pastoral, as well as to some pathetic scenes in Homer's *Odyssey*, the Greek romance is usually concerned with chaste young royal lovers who undergo innumerable misfortunes such as abduction and shipwreck, and who finally are united in marriage. The emphasis is on plot (the characters are merely virtuous or merely vicious), and there are stories within stories as the lovers seek each other, sometimes in disguise, often in exotic lands. (Consult M. Hadas, ed. *Three Greek Romances.*) The Middle Ages, too, had their romances, tales in *lingua Romanica* (*i.e.*, in the vernacular, rather than in Latin). Such tales, at first in verse, later in prose, described exciting adventures – usually of separated lovers – in strange lands where the marvelous abounds. The anonymous *Sir Gawain and the Green Knight* includes a green man who survives decapitation. The romance, with its emphasis on the unusual, commonly is less interested in the observable details of ordinary life and in "real" characters than in adventure, and often its strange happenings seem to hint at °allegory. (Consult G. Highet, *The Classical Tradition;* D. Everett, *Essays on Middle English Literature;* and L. Hibbard, *Medieval Romance in England.*)

In Italy during the later Middle Ages and the °Renaissance, a short prose tale, whether serious or comic, was called a ***novella*** ("a short new thing," "news"). In the seventeenth and eighteenth centuries a novel commonly was a short tale of love, "a kind of abbreviation of a romance," but during the nineteenth century it was common to separate the "romance" from the "novel" on the basis of the probability of the setting or background. Hawthorne, for example, in his preface to *The House of the Seven Gables,* distinguishes thus between romance and novel: "The latter form of composition is presumed to aim at a very minute fidelity, not merely to the possible, but to the probable and ordinary course of man's experience. The former – while, as a work of art, it must rigidly subject itself to laws, and while it sins unpardonably so far as it may swerve aside from the truth of the human heart – has fairly a right to present that truth under circumstances, to a great extent, of the writer's own choosing or creation." In his preface to *The Marble Fawn,* Hawthorne explains that he chose "Italy as the site of his Romance" because it afforded him "a sort of poetic or fairy precinct, where actualities would not be so terribly insisted upon as they are . . . in America." We associate the novel with believable details because it matured in the eighteenth century, when much literature, in response to the demand of the rising middle class for verisimilitude, sought to give the impression of history. Mary McCarthy, in *On the Contrary,* emphasizes the apparent "reality" of the novel. She argues that if a long prose work has talking animals in it, the book is not a novel but a fable.

The novel may be °tragic, °comic, °satiric, etc., though if it is satiric and the emphasis is not on story and character (see °plot), it may be better to classify it simply as a satire. *Gulliver's Travels* is a long prose narrative, yet it is not a novel. Gulliver's journeys are not really the substance of the book but are the loose narrative which contains a dissection of all sorts of extremes of human behavior. He meets Lilliputians, giants, and rational horses, but the emphasis is less on narrative and/or on character development than on the anatomizing of human folly. A fundamentally different sort of travel story is the **picaresque novel,** presenting the exploits of a rogue (Spanish *pícaro:* rogue). The picaresque novel is usually a detailed satiric picture of middle-class life, in which a roguish but engaging fellow tells of the shrewd shifts by which he triumphs over the less bright members of the bourgeoisie whom he encounters. Because the form originated in sixteenth-century Spain as a kind of °burlesque of tales of chivalric adventures, the *pícaro* wins in one situation after another, and the novel has an episodic structure (see °episode). Examples are Smollett's *The Adventures of Roderick Random* and Mark Twain's *Adventures of Huckleberry Finn.* (For a suggestive discussion, especially of Thomas Mann's *The Confessions of Felix Krull,* consult R. B. Heilman, "Variations of Picaresque," *The Sewannee Review,* 66 [1958], 547–77; and R. Alter, *Rogue's Progress.*) Although almost all novels have (like the picaresque) a fairly concrete setting (*e.g.,* along the Mississippi, c. 1850), if the setting includes historical persons (Napoleon) or if the setting (French Revolution) is drawn in such detail that the reader feels that the period as well as the characters are the novelist's subject, then the novel may be termed a **historical novel.** Dickens's *A Tale of Two Cities,* wherein no historical figure appears, can be called a historical novel by virtue of its emphasis on the setting (revolutionary France), but usually some historical figures move in the background (*e.g.,* Napoleon in Tolstoi's *War and Peace*). In recent decades, historical figures have played larger roles in novels, but such works (*e.g.,* Robert Graves's *I, Claudius* and Sholem Asch's *The Nazarene*) might well be termed "fictional biographies" or romances.

The ***roman à clef*** (French for "novel with a key") uses contemporary historical figures as its chief characters, but they are disguised with fictitious names. In Aldous Huxley's *Point Counter Point,* Mark Rampion is modeled on D. H. Lawrence. The ***Bildungsroman,*** or ***Erziehungsroman*** (German for "novel of development"), deals with maturation, wherein the hero becomes "civilized" – *i.e.,* becomes aware of himself as he relates to the objective world outside of his subjective consciousness. Notable examples are Goethe's *Wilhelm Meister* and Thomas Mann's *The Magic Mountain.* When the *Bildungsroman* is concerned specifically with the development of the artist, as are Samuel Butler's *The Way of All Flesh* and James Joyce's *A Portrait of* *the Artist as a Young Man,* it is sometimes termed a ***Künstlerroman*** (German for "novel of the artist"). A novel that pays great attention to the complicated mental states of its characters (as the *Künstlerroman* often does) is a **psychological novel.** Though psychological fiction is at least a century old (Dostoevski), in the twentieth century exploration of the levels of mental activity has increased. A notable kind of psychological novel is the **stream of consciousness novel** ("stream of consciousness" is a °metaphor coined in 1890 by William James in *Principles of Psychology* to describe the flux of thought), which records mental activity ranging from complete consciousness to unconsciousness. Its most prominent technique is the **interior monologue,** which reveals the minds of characters and presents not overt actions and speech or even thoughts in logical and grammatical order; rather, it attempts to present what has been called the mind's "pre-speech levels of consciousness" in such a manner (commonly without punctuation, logical transitions, or conventional syntax, and with little or no intervention by the author) as to suggest the fluid and unending activity of the mind, with all its apparent irrelevant associations. Joyce's *Ulysses* is a stream of consciousness novel; its last forty-six pages, an uninterrupted flow of Molly Bloom's thoughts, are an interior monologue. But words printed one after the other on a page cannot, of course, precisely duplicate the welter of thoughts which – without even being verbalized – pass through the mind. The interior monologue, then, is quite as °conventional as, say, the °soliloquy. (Consult R. Humphrey, *Stream of Consciousness in the Modern Novel;* and M. Friedman, *Stream of Consciousness.* See °short story, °point of view, °plot, and epistolary novel [under °epistle]. On the novel in general, consult E. Baker, *The History of the English Novel* [12 vols.]; I. Watt, *The Rise of the Novel;* A. C. Kettle, *An Introduction to the English Novel* [2 vols.]; D. Daiches, *The Novel and the Modern World;* R. Liddell, *Some Principles of Fiction,* and his *A Treatise on the Novel,* reissued in one volume as *Robert Liddell on the Novel;* M. McCarthy, *On the Contrary;* P. Lubbock, *The Craft of Fiction;* E. M. Forster, *Aspects of the Novel;* and W. Allen, *The English Novel.* For a study of all kinds of narrative [epic, romance, novel, etc.] consult R. Scholes and R. Kellogg, *The Nature of Narrative.*)

nuntius. See °tragedy.

novelette. See °novel.

novella. See °novel.

objective. See °subjective.

objective correlative. T. S. Eliot, in "Hamlet and His Problems" (1919), made current the phrase, explaining that in order to express an emotion in art, an artist must find an "objective correlative," that is, "a set of objects, a situation, a chain of events which shall be the formula of that *particular* emotion" and which then will evoke the emotion in the reader. Eliot says that "the state of mind of Lady Macbeth walking in her sleep has been communicated to you by a skilful accumulation of imagined sensory impressions." Eliot apparently means that the poem is an organization which stands for the poet's emotion, and the poem evokes this same emotion in the reader. (For numerous comments on the term, consult *The Critic's Notebook,* ed. R. W. Stallman. Eliot himself seems to reject the idea in the introduction to his *The Use of Poetry and the Use of Criticism* and in "The Perfect Critic," in *The Sacred Wood.*)

occasional poem. A poem written for a particular occasion; *e.g.*, Milton's °sonnet, "On the Late Massacre in Piemont."

octave. See °versification.

octavo. See °folio.

octometer and **octosyllabic couplet.** See °versification.

ode. Originally a song in honor of gods or heroes, now commonly a °lyric poem – usually of considerable length – characterized by lofty feeling (see °hymn). Pindar (c. 522–443 B.C.), a Greek, wrote odes that were choral celebrations of athletic prowess and nobility, often linking the hero with divine legends. Pindar's odes commonly consist of several °stanzas, each stanza containing three parts: a **strophe** (wherein the chorus danced a pattern while singing), an **antistrophe** (wherein the chorus retraced the pattern while singing), and an **epode** (wherein perhaps the chorus sang without dancing). Within these divisions are lines of uneven length, and subsequent odes have frequently imitated the irregular appearance as well as the great passion of the **Pindaric ode.** Some imitations catch the irregularity but not the elaborate stanzaic pattern, and the result is the **Cowleyan ode** (named for Abraham Cowley), an ode with no regular repeated pattern. Notable English Pindarics, influenced by the Cowleyan tradition, are Gray's "The Progress of Poesy" and Wordsworth's "Ode: Intimations of Immortality." In Rome, Horace (65–8 B.C.) wrote quieter odes than Pindar, usually celebrating love, patriotism, or simple Roman morality in stanzas of four lines. Notable English **Horatian odes** are Marvell's "Horatian Ode upon Cromwell's Return from Ireland," and Collins's "Ode to Evening." Although the ode is a serious poem expressing the speaker's passion – often admiration or wonder – the object of this passion may be almost anything; especially during the °Romantic Movement (see °classic and romantic), the ode tended to become less public and more personal and introspective. Cf. Shelley's "Ode to the West Wind," or Keats's odes to a nightingale, to autumn, on a Grecian urn, and on melancholy. (Consult G. Highet, *The Classical Tradition,* Ch. 12; C. Maddison, *Apollo and the Nine;* and J. F. A. Heath-Stubbs, *The Ode.*)

Old Comedy. See °comedy.

onomatopoeia. See °versification.

oral transmission. See °ballad, °epic, °folklore, and °saga.

organic unity. See °unity.

ottava rima. See °versification.

oxymoron. See °figurative language.

palindrome. A reversible word (example: level) or line. Examples: "Madam, I'm Adam" (to which Eve palindromically replied, "Eve"); "A man, a plan, a canal – Panama." (Consult C. C. Bombaugh, *Oddities and Curiosities,* pp. 59–63, 342–46.)

palinode. A poem written to retract something said in a previous poem.

pan shot. See °shot.

pantomime. See °drama.

parable. See °allegory.

paradox. Usually a statement or situation that seems – but need not be – self-contradictory. When in one of his "Holy Sonnets" John Donne wishes his proud spirit broken so that he may achieve salvation, he appeals to God paradoxically; "That I may rise and stand, o'erthrow me." Cleanth Brooks, in *The Well-Wrought Urn,* has given the word a place in critical terminology by maintaining that paradox is "the language appropriate and inevitable to poetry" in contrast to the nonparadoxical or explicit language of science. Poetry, Brooks holds, works "by contradiction and qualification," by °metaphors (see °figurative language) wherein there are "necessary overlappings, discrepancies, contradictions." See °irony, and (under °figurative language) °oxymoron, which is a condensed paradox.

parallelism. See °form.

paraphrase. See °form.

parody. See °burlesque.

paronomasia. See °figurative language.

particular. See °concrete.

pastoral. Any writing having to do with shepherds may be called pastoral literature. Theocritus (third century B.C.), a Greek, wrote pastoral poems about Sicilian herdsmen, and some of his themes (*e.g.*, a singing match between shepherds, a shepherd lamenting his mistress's coldness, an °elegy for a dead shepherd) have been widely used by later poets, including Vergil, Spenser, and Milton. Pastorals are often set in °Arcadia (see under °Golden Age), a mountainous district of Greece, proverbial for its peaceful shepherds who lived a simple happy life. Singing and wooing are the chief pastoral activities; and such is the power of the tradition that a "swain" (herdsman) has come to mean a lover. A pastoral poem can also be called a **bucolic** or an °**idyll** or an **eclogue.** (An idyll is sometimes a miniature and picturesque °epic, as Tennyson's *Idylls of the King;* an eclogue is commonly a °dialogue between shepherds, yet sometimes it is any dialogue where some attention is also paid to setting.)

In general, ancient poets after Theocritus depicted rural life as unsullied and therefore superior to urban life. Christian poets have sometimes fused the Greco-Roman tradition with the Hebrew-Christian tradition of the shepherd as the holy man (cf. David, the shepherd who sang psalms, and Christ as the Good Shepherd), thus enlarging the form. Renato Poggioli suggests (*Harvard Library Bulletin,* XI [1957], 147–74, to be included in a forthcoming book) that despite these points of contact between the shepherd of sheep and the Shepherd of Souls, the pastoral is essentially un-Christian, for it celebrates the satisfaction of desires whereas Christianity insists on some degree of mortification of the flesh. Thus, Poggioli says, the Christian pastoral uses its shepherds merely °satirically or °allegorically (say, the shepherd as priest, the wolf as devil, or as false priest, etc.), but is essentially unpastoral in its ideology. The **georgic** is a poem dealing with rural life, especially with farming; unlike the pastoral, it usually depicts a life of labor rather than of singing and dancing. (See °Golden Age and °primitivism. Consult W. W. Greg, *Pastoral Poetry and Pastoral Drama;* J. F. A. Heath-Stubbs, *The Pastoral;* G. Highet, *The Classical Tradition;* H. Smith, *Elizabethan Poetry;* and J. Chalker, *The English Georgic.*)

pathetic fallacy. See °personification (under °figurative language).

pathos. The quality in a work that evokes sympathy or sorrow or pity. The pathetic is often distinguished from the tragic; in the former, the suffering is experienced by the passive and the innocent (especially women and children), while in the latter it is experienced by persons who act, struggle, and are at least in some small measure responsible for their sufferings. Discussing Aeschylus's *The Suppliants,* H. D. F. Kitto says in *Greek Tragedy* (2nd ed.): "The Suppliants are not only pathetic, as the victims of outrage, but also tragic, as the victims of their own misconceptions." Pathos must also be distinguished from **bathos.** Though "bathos" was Greek for "depth" or "profundity," Alexander Pope fixed its modern meaning in his *Peri-Bathous, or the Art of Sinking in Poetry* (1728) wherein he ridicules poets for sudden descents from the sublime. Bathos is either (1) pathos so overdone that it evokes laughter rather than pity, or (2) a sudden drop to the trivial, producing an undesired ludicrous effect. An example of the first sort is Dickens's description of the death of Little Nell in *The Old Curiosity Shop.* (Oscar Wilde said of this death-scene that only a man with a heart of stone could read it without laughing.) An example of the second sort of bathos is this passage from Wordsworth's "Address to My Infant Daughter":

> — Hast thou then survived —
> Mild offspring of infirm humanity,
> Meek infant! among all forlornest things
> The most forlorn — one life of that bright star,
> The second glory of the Heavens? — Thou hast. . . .

If the drop is for a desired comic effect, the device is called °anticlimax rather than bathos. (For a collection of bathetic poetry, see *The Stuffed Owl,* ed. D. B. Wyndham Lewis and C. Lee.)

pentameter. See °versification.

periodic sentence. See °style.

peripeteia (or **peripety**). See °tragedy and °plot.

periphrasis. Commonly defined as a circumlocution, periphrasis (such as "whiskered vermin race" for "rats," or "a stercoraceous heap" for "a manure pile") would seem to be pointless wordiness. But an indirect way of stating something may sometimes be the best way of stating it. Thus, when Pope speaks of the "sea" as a "wat'ry plain," he calls attention to a particular attribute or property (in this example, expansiveness). Similarly, "fleecy wealth" for "sheep" says more than "sheep." Old English poetry makes use of **kennings,** stereotyped synonyms ("prince of rings" for "ruler") or compound words or phrases with some °metaphoric (see °figurative language) value, such as "whale-road" for "sea," "foamy floater" for "ship," and "life's house" for "body." In "Morte d'Arthur" Tennyson imitated the device, speaking of "moving isles of winter" (icebergs) and of "drops of onset" (blood). In the eighteenth century a common periphrasis was an °epithet and a generic term, such as "plumy band" for "birds," or "finny tribe" for "fish." (Consult G. Tillotson, *Augustan Poetic Diction.*)

persona (plural: **personae**). (1) The character or characters in a piece, especially in a °drama. (2) Recently the word has been applied to what has also been called the **voice** (or **mask**) speaking in any work. The speaker is not the author but the author's creation. It may be a duke who is speaking, as in Browning's "My Last Duchess." But even a °lyric is spoken by a "persona" rather than by the poet at his desk. Robert Burns wrote "John Anderson, My Jo," but the persona who speaks is John's old wife. The persona has an attitude toward his subject, himself, and his audience. Thus, a persona in a particular poem may be a happy lover anxious to share his joy, an unhappy lover confessing his sorrow to himself alone, etc. The "I," that is, is not the writer but a created voice such as the unfeeling economist through whose mouth Swift sets forth "A Modest Proposal." Gulliver, too, is a persona. (See °tone. Consult G. T. Wright, *The Poet in the Poem;* and I. Ehrenpreis, "Personae," *Restoration and Eighteenth-Century Literature,* ed. C. Camden.)

personification. See °figurative language.

Petrarchan. See °sonnet (under °versification), and °metaphysical poetry.

picaresque novel. See °novel.

pièce bien faite (or **well-made play**). A play, with much °suspense and with little depth of characterization, that relies on a cleverly constructed plot, first developing a situation, then building the crisis to a climax, and then resolving the business. The type, perhaps it can be described as °melodrama with the fisticuffs left out, is chiefly associated with Victorien Sardou (1831–1908), but Sardou was indebted to Eugène Scribe (1791–1861). Shaw called their plays clockwork mice and Sardoodledom, but the influence of Sardou on Shaw's hero, Ibsen, is undeniable. (See °plot. Consult Walter Kerr, *How Not to Write a Play,* Ch. 10; Eric Bentley, "Homage to Scribe," *What is Theatre?;* C. E. Montague, *Dramatic Values,* pp. 63–74; and *Camille and Other Plays,* ed. Stephen S. Stanton.)

Platonism, Platonic love, and **neoplatonism.** Plato held that the visible world derives whatever reality it has from an invisible world of Forms or Ideas. The invisible world is studied through man's reason or his intellect. The theory of Platonic love, discussed notably in Plato's *Symposium,* holds that the lover of beauty ought not to rest content with the vision of beauty in a single mortal, but ought to rise to a higher step on the stairway of love and love all physical beauty. He will then be able to rise yet another step to the vision of the beauty of the soul, then to the beauty of institutions, then to the beauty of the sciences (*i.e.*, intellectual beauty), and finally he ought to rise to an intellectual vision of the eternal unchanging Idea of Beauty, of which beautiful mortals (physical beauty) partake only crudely and temporarily. Furthermore, the soul of the Platonic lover who had achieved this vision could engender beautiful conceptions in the soul of his beloved. The **neoplatonists** of the third century A.D. attempted to fuse aspects of Platonic, Hebrew, Christian, and Near Eastern mystical thought. They held that the material world was a dim manifestation or creation of Infinite Being; Infinite Being was perfectly good and could not be known through the senses or reason. This **neoplatonism** was contemptuous of the material world – the world of the sense – but regarded man highly, valuing not his senses or even his reason but a suprarational divine quality in him. However, °Renaissance neoplatonists, notably Ficino and Pico della Mirandola in fifteenth-century Florence, were far from contemptuous of the material world; they argued that because the reality of the material consists of the spiritual, man can approach the spiritual through the material. Later in the Renaissance the doctrine was commonly somewhat perverted, and a Renaissance Platonic lover could engage his heart to fleshly beauty and assure himself that he was, in neoplatonic style, reverencing the spiritual beauty that dwelt in a fleshly mansion. Edmund Spenser in his "Epithalamion" describes his bride's bodily beauty, and then says:

> But if ye saw that which no eyes can see,
> The inward beauty of her lively sprite,
> Garnisht with heavenly gifts of high degree,
> Much more then would ye wonder at that sight.

(Consult A. E. Taylor, *Plato;* G. M. Grube, *Plato's Thought;* and [for neoplatonism] H. Baker, *The Dignity of Man,* reprinted as *The Image of Man.*)

plot — story — character. Distinctions between "plot" and "story" vary widely, but for many critics **story** is the sequence in which events occur as parts of a happening and **plot** is the sequence in which the author arranges (narrates or dramatizes) them. The story of *Paradise Lost,* for example, tells of the rebellion in heaven by Satan and his followers, their defeat at God's hand, their fall, and the consequent revenge they took on God by seducing Adam and Eve. But Milton begins his poem with the rebellious angels already in hell (°*in medias res*), and later he shows how they arrived there. The plot of *Paradise Lost* is the narrative structure (arrangement of episodes) that Milton presents, but the story is the episodes in chronological order. An interruption in the chronological arrangement, presenting an earlier episode than the one that has just been presented, is a **flashback** or **retrospect.** Critics often distinguish between those parts of a °novel that are **scene** and those that are **summary.** A scene shows things happening; it often has °dialogue, and it always gives the impression of careful representation, whether of words, thoughts, or gestures. The following sample miniature scene is from *David Copperfield:* "Mrs. Joram tossed her head, endeavoring to be very stern and cross; but she could not command her softer self, and began to cry." A summary, on the other hand, briefly conveys necessary but relatively unimportant information, and it does not give the effect of representation. This sample miniature summary is also from *David Copperfield:* "He soon became known to every boy in the school."

Aristotle's use of plot (Greek *mythos,* sometimes translated as "fable") is a little uncertain: in Chapter 5 of the *Poetics,* his treatise on literature, he speaks of plots as "unified stories"; in Chapter 6 he call plot "the whole structure of the incidents," and he speaks of plot as the "soul of tragedy," thus making it more important than character. By **character** he means the personalities of the figures in the story. A story, according to Aristotle, is not necessarily unified. For example, Homer's *Iliad* has for its story the Trojan War, but this story includes innumerable episodes that have only slight connections between them, and Homer therefore omitted many episodes. He chose as his subject an underlying **action:** the wrath of Achilles and the destruction it caused. The wrath of Achilles manifests itself in various activities, but not all the activities of the Trojan War are manifestations of this wrath, and Homer omits those that are not such manifestations. According to Aristotle, the writer keeps his eye on a unified action, and selects and rearranges parts of the story into a plot. This underlying unified action often expresses itself in external physical actions or deeds (Achilles slays Hector), but the underlying action is action even if not physically expressed. The wrath of Achilles may, that is, express itself in a deed, in a speech, or even in refusal to act. In short, Aristotle's "action" or "doings" includes not only physical expressions but also inner states of being, as in our phrase, "How are you doing?" For an action to have °unity, according to Aristotle (Ch. 8), "the events of which it is made up must be so plotted that if any of these elements is moved or removed the whole is altered and upset. For when a thing can be included or not included without making any noticeable difference, that thing is no part of the whole." Some critics substitute the word "theme" for "action," but "theme" is often used for the thesis or "message" of a didactic work. "Action" in this sense is virtually identical with "meaning," if one grants that the meaning of a work of art is not a detachable message but is embodied in all of the details of the work.

To return to the relation of plot to character: for Aristotle, the aspects of personality (whether a warrior is brave or cowardly, gentle or harsh, etc.) arise out of the action the writer has in mind. Menander (a Greek comic dramatist) is said to have told a friend that he had finished a comedy, though he had not yet written a line of it; the anecdote implies that Menander had completed his idea of *what happens* (action) and in *what order* (plot), and he would find it easy then to write the lines of the characters necessary to this plot. The separation, however, between plot and character is misleading, for the two usually interplay. Although it is true that there may be much plot and little character (as in a thriller), in most works of art there is such a fusion between what is done and the personality of the doer that we feel the truth of Henry James's questions: "What is character but the determination of incident? What is incident but the illustration of character?" (On plot and character, consult R. Scholes and R. Kellogg, *The Nature of Narrative*, Chs. 5 and 6.)

When character largely determines what is done (the incident), there is **motivation.** Although in some works a god or equivalent (Fortune, Chance) intervenes and determines the happenings, most often what happens is the plausible outcome of a character's personality. If a character does things that seem inappropriate to his personality and his situation, he is said to be poorly motivated. Characters are sometimes divided into **flat** and **round characters.** The former (common in Dickens) have only one "side," representing a single trait (*e.g.*, the faithful wife, the genial drunkard), whereas the latter have many traits and are seen, as it were, from all sides, in the round. The behavior of flat characters is thoroughly predictable; that of round characters is sometimes unexpected though always credible. The term "flat" is not necessarily pejorative, for it is sometimes desirable to show only one aspect of a single character. Indeed, Western narratives were scarcely concerned with either rounded or developing characters until the Middle Ages. An °epic hero, for example, is fairly flat, and at the end he is much as he was at the beginning. In such narratives, the concern is with his heroic actions, rather than with his complexities or with his growth.

Most plots entail a **conflict,** wherein the hero (**protagonist**) is somehow opposed. If he is opposed chiefly by a second person rather than by a force such as Fate or God or by an aspect of himself, the opposing figure is the **antagonist.** A **foil** is a contrast, specifically, a character who sets off another. Laertes and Fortinbras, like Hamlet, are fatherless young men, but each behaves differently and thus is a foil to the others. The German critic, Gustav Freytag, in *Technique of the Drama* (1863), held that a play dramatizes "the rushing forth of will power from the depths of man's soul toward the external world," and "the coming into being of a deed and its consequences on the human soul." The five-act play, he said, commonly arranged such an action into a **pyramidal structure,** consisting of a **rising action,** a **climax,** and a **falling action.** Though he applied his formula mechanically, his terminology has been found useful for discussing not only some °dramas but also some °short stories and °novels. The rising action begins with an **exposition** (presentation of essential information, especially about what has occurred before this piece of action began), and rises through a **complication** (the protagonist is opposed) to a high point or **crisis** or **climax** (a moment at which tension is high, and which is a decisive turning point). The falling action goes through a **reversal** (if a °tragedy, the protagonist loses power), and then into a **catastrophe,** also called a **dénouement** (unknotting) or **resolution.** (The reversal, which Aristotle called ***peripeteia*** and which is sometimes Anglicized to **peripety,** would in a comedy be a change from bad fortune to good, and the catastrophe would thus be happy.) The dénouement frequently involves what Aristotle called ***anagnorisis*** (**recognition, disclosure, discovery**). This recognition may be as simple as the identification of a long-lost brother by a birthmark, or it may involve a character's recognition of his own true condition. (See °tragedy, and °suspense.)

Some works have a **double plot;** that is, two plots, usually with some sort of interrelation (*e.g.,* parallel or contrasting). For example, the **subplot** or **underplot** might be a grotesque version of the serious main plot (*e.g.,* Shakespeare's *The Tempest*). In *King Lear,* the main plot concerns Lear's relation to his daughters and the subplot concerns the Duke of Gloucester's relation to his sons. For other aspects of the subplot, see °comic relief, °unity, and °atmosphere.

poète maudit. See °classic and romantic.

poetic diction. See °epithet, °periphrasis, and, especially, °diction.

poetic justice. A term introduced into England by Thomas Rymer in 1678, denoting the reward of the virtuous and the punishment of the vicious. Aristotle had said or implied that the tragic hero is undone partly by some sort of personal flaw – *i.e.*, he is at least partly responsible for the suffering he later encounters. (See °*hamartia*, under °tragedy.) "Poetic justice," with its idea that all characters reap the harvest of their just deserts, is a hardening of Aristotle's suggestion. It is easily seen in Nahum Tate's revision (1681) of *King Lear*, wherein not only do the villians die but the heroes live. Lear is restored to his throne, and Cordelia weds Edgar. (Consult M. A. Quinlan, *Poetic Justice in the Drama;* and W. K. Wimsatt, Jr., and C. Brooks, *Literary Criticism.*)

poetic license. A writer's privilege to depart from some expected standard. This license, though it originally covered all deviations from standards expected in prose (*e.g.*, rhyme, inversion in word order), came to be applied to deviations that are faults. °Anachronisms were often thus excused. The term is rarely used today, however, since it is now assumed that faults are faults.

poetry. See °literature, °versification, °figurative language, and the separate types, such as °elegy, °lyric, °ode.

point of view. A piece of literature (*i.e.*, poem, short story, novel) is told or recorded by someone, and this narrator has a particular identity. The story is rarely told by the artist speaking in his own personality; usually it is told through an assumed "point of view," an assumed eye and mind (a °persona).

Points of view can be divided into first and third person. The teller of a first-person point of view can be a **first-person observer** of a tale about Jones ("I last met Jones in 1922") or a **first-person participant** – Jones or his wife ("I had just got married, and was looking for a house"). If the first-person narrator is naive (a child, a not-too-bright adult, an idiot) and the tale is filtered through his uncomprehending mind, the point of view is usually called the **innocent eye.** (Notable innocent eyes are: the barber in Ring Lardner's "Haircut," who chatters about a local accident that the reader understands was in fact a murder; Benjy, the thirty-three-year-old idiot who narrates the first part of Faulkner's *The Sound and the Fury;* and Lemmuel Gulliver, who tells of his travels.) A first-person point of view normally involves some degree of ironic distance between the narrator and the author (Gulliver, for example, is on the whole a rather simple fellow, not at all like Swift, and the reader presumably shares Swift's view of Gulliver.) Third-person points of view are commonly divided into omniscient, selective omniscient, and objective. In the **omniscient point of view,** the voice narrating the tale can record the thoughts of all the characters ("John was lonely, but didn't perceive that Mary was lonely too"). The oral °epic customarily is told by an omniscient narrator: he sees all and knows all. If the voice comments on the story ("Loneliness has its pleasures as well as its pains," or "But, dear readers, we must not be upset by the loneliness of these puppets"), it exemplifies **editorial omniscience.** Many modern critics are distressed by such editorializing; they tend to identify the narrator with the author, and they feel that the author should be less in evidence and more willing to let us interpret the story for ourselves. If the voice abstains from editorializing and merely records, it exemplifies **neutral omniscience.** If the voice enters into the mind of only one character, or very few, the point of view exemplifies **selective omniscience** (also called **limited omniscience**). If the voice does not editorialize and does not enter into the minds of any of the characters, but simply records what is visible ("John looked at Mary. She looked away"), it is an **objective point of view,** sometimes called "fly-on-the-wall," or "the camera." The point of view from which a tale is told can be highly complex: in Conrad's *Heart of Darkness*, an unnamed narrator tells us the tale that Marlow told him, and Marlow in fact often told the narrator what others had told Marlow. (For a thorough history and analysis, consult N. Friedman, "Point of View in Fiction," *Publications of the Modern Language Association*, 70 [1955], 1160–84; W. C. Booth, *The Rhetoric of Fiction*, Ch. 6.)

portmanteau word. See °figurative language.

primitivism. The doctrine that civilization in some ways worsens men, and that, therefore, men in simple "natural" societies are superior to men in complex "artificial" societies. For example, it has been said that the shepherd's life is free from the cares and vices of the urban man's life. Primitivism presupposes some sort of natural goodness in man – instinct, reason, imagination – and assumes that civilization (which is man-made) corrupts this goodness. Primitivism is commonly divided into: (1) **chronological primitivism,** which assumes that the earlier stages in the history of a people were better than the present stage (*i.e.*, "the good old days" were best, or medieval feudal life was better than modern industrial life, or the child is superior to the man);

and (2) **cultural primitivism,** which assumes that some peoples of the present represent an earlier, better, and more "natural" stage of society (contemporary shepherds, South Sea Islanders). Hemingway's glorification of active, strong-feeling men (fishermen, bullfighters, hunters) smacks of cultural primitivism, and is close to the idea of the **noble savage** as stated by Dryden in *The Conquest of Granada* (1670):

> I am as free as nature first made man,
> Ere the base laws of servitude began,
> When wild in woods the noble savage ran.

In short, primitivism opposes belief in progress; at best it hopes that man can progress (or regress) to a state wherein he regains a lost past; and it generally finds its ideal in remote times or places. (See °classic, °Golden Age, and °pastoral. Consult A. O. Lovejoy and G. Boas, *Primitivism . . . in Antiquity;* L. Whitney, *Primitivism and Ideas of Progress;* and O. Cargill, *Intellectual America.*)

problem play. See °drama.

projective poetry. Largely associated with Charles Olson (1910–70), who held that a projective poem has no clearly defined limits, for it is shaped by the internal relations of its parts rather than by a conventional poetic form such as the sonnet. Olson quotes Edward Dahlberg: "One perception must immediately and directly lead to a further perception." The effect in the poetry of Olson and Robert Creeley commonly is of sharply perceptive lines linked by the poet's associations, and the poem tends at last to stop rather than to come to completion. (Consult Charles Olson, "Projective Verse," in *The New American Poetry, 1945–1960*, ed. Donald M. Allen [1960].)

prologue. (1) A preface or introduction, especially to a °drama. (2) The actor who speaks a preface to a drama.

prose. See °literature, °style, °versification (for rhythmic prose), and such types as °novel, °short story, °essay.

prosody. See °versification.

prosopopoeia. Personification; see °figurative language.

protagonist. See °plot.

proverb. See °aphorism.

psychical distance (or **aesthetic distance**). The detachment between the receptor and the work of art. The concept is chiefly associated with Edward Bullough (see the essay in his *Aesthetics*, reprinted in M. Rader, *A Modern Book of Esthetics*, and, in part, in E. Vivas and M. Krieger, *Problems of Aesthetics*). Bullough explains that there must be some sort of "distance" (gap) between our practical self (our personal needs) and the work of art. Thus, a jealous man who suspects his wife will have difficulty divorcing his personal feelings from *Othello*. He will be too involved with the piece as life to see it as art. But notice that "distance" does not mean that the receptor is totally detached or objective. Rather, he is detached from his usual personal involvements, and precisely because of this detachment he can look with a new vigorous interest – he can look with a new sort of passion born of his new personality – at the work of art as art. Persons who do not understand the need for distance between themselves and a work, Bullough explains, commonly say that they do not wish to see a °tragedy because there is enough suffering in real life. But the more sophisticated spectator at a tragedy realizes that, just as the frame around a picture and the pedestal under a statue induce distance, the play is distanced (the characters may speak verse, they perform behind footlights, and their deeds cohere to make a unified harmonious pattern) and that the feelings it evokes in him are not at all the feelings evoked by a roughly similar event in real life. At a tragedy we feel "rapturous awe" at what in life would be depressing. Similarly, when we look at a sculpture of a human form, the stone is sufficiently different from flesh to "distance" the piece, and we become highly interested in it, but not at all in the practical way we would become interested in looking at the live model who posed for the statue. See °dramatic illusion.

pun. See °figurative language.

pure poetry. See °didactic literature.

puritanism. In the sixteenth century a faction of Protestantism that set out to purify the Anglican Church of all traces of Roman Catholicism, returning the Church to a simple form of worship. D. Bush, in *English Literature in the Earlier Seventeenth Century*, page 7, says, "The word Puritan . . . properly denotes firm adherence to the Bible as the sole and sufficient authority in all matters of ecclesiastical government and ceremony as well as of belief and conduct." In the seventeenth century, Puritans were identified with those who were hostile to the festive and the fictive aspects of the arts. It is true that many Puritans were especially hostile to popular drama, romance, and folk customs such as May celebrations with songs of wooing, but it is not true that they universally scorned the arts. (One has only to recall that John Milton was a Puritan.) They especially seem to have cultivated music, perhaps because it is the least representative, least didactic art and therefore it competes least with the Word; and they were interested in biography and autobiography because these modes perpetuated the memory of ideal religious lives. Although they distrusted eloquence, and favored a relatively plain °style in their sermons, they allowed that eloquence coupled with "evidence of the spirit" was valuable. (Consult L. Sasek, *The Literary Temper of the English Puritans.*) During the **Puritan Interregnum**, or Commonwealth Period (from the end of the Civil War in 1649 until the Restoration of Charles II in 1660), England was ruled by Parliament rather than by a monarch. The theaters were closed throughout this period, though there were some surreptitious performances.

purple passage. A florid or ornate portion of prose or poetry, which stands out by its °rhythm (see °versification), °diction, or °figurative language. The term, frequently derogatory, need not be. An example is the description of Queen Mab's chariot in *Romeo and Juliet:*

> Her waggon-spokes made of long spinners' legs,
> The cover of the wings of grasshoppers,
> Her traces of the smallest spider web,
> Her collars of the moonshine's watery beams,
> Her whip of cricket's bone, the lash of film,
> Her waggoner a small grey-coated gnat,
> Not half so big as a round little worm
> Prick'd from the lazy finger of a maid.

pyrrhic. See °versification.

quantitative verse. See °versification.

quarto. See °folio.

quatrain. See °versification.

raisonneur. See °chorus.

realism. The detailed presentation of appearances, especially of familiar experiences and circumstances. The French painter Gustave Courbet (1819–77) called himself a "realist" because he painted life as (he claimed) it shows itself to be, filled not with nymphs, swains, and exotic figures, but with dirty working men. Literature has from earliest times occasionally included careful descriptions of middle- and low-class life, but "realism" is the name applied to a movement in the nineteenth century that presented descriptions of observed details of every-day life. William Dean Howells, a notable realist, said that realism sought "to front the every-day world and catch the charm of its work-worn, care-worn, brave, kindly face." This movement, with its affection for the common world, was sometimes closely allied to the **local color movement,** which dwelt on picturesque details (usually scenery, quaint customs, and dialect) characteristic of a particular region. Though often °sentimental, when local color went beyond an infatuation with externals and penetrated to character, it was an important aspect of realism. Especially after the Civil War, American realists (notably Mark Twain, Stephen Crane, and Hamlin Garland) showed a note of disillusion not found in Howells, depicting little people as having a full share of little vices. In its humble subject-matter, realism shows its debt to °romanticism (see °classic and romantic), but realism, claiming to record life as it passes the window, generally avoids the romantic interest in the mysterious, in the exotic, in the depths of the abnormal imagination which are beneath the simple appearances – *i.e.*, it avoids what Wordsworth called "strange seas of thought." Realism should not be confused with °naturalism, which generally implies a deterministic view of man. (Consult A. Kazin, *On Native Grounds*; and H. Levin, *Contexts of Criticism*.)

recognition. See °plot and °tragedy.

refrain. See °ballad and °versification.

Renaissance. (From French, for "rebirth.") The alleged rebirth of learning and art in the fourteenth and fifteenth centuries in Italy and France and in the sixteenth century in England. The learning that was reborn was supposedly that of the Greeks and Romans, and if rebirth is not quite the right word, it is nevertheless true that some ancient writings (especially Greek) unknown to the Middle Ages were discovered, and that the development in Europe (c. 1450) of printing by movable type on paper allowed learning to be widely disseminated. The idea of a rebirth after a sterile millennium was originated by the Italian writers of the period and still survives. The Renaissance is usually characterized as a glorious period of individualism when creative energy flourished and religious tyranny faded, but scholars have increasingly come to see, first, that many aspects of the Renaissance are rooted in the Middle Ages, and, second, that medieval achievements were considerable. An extreme version of this second view, held mostly by Roman Catholics, is that the Renaissance lost much that was good in medievalism, and created nothing new of value. Etienne Gilson says, "The Renaissance . . . was not the Middle Ages plus man, but the Middle Ages minus God, and the tragedy is that in losing God the Renaissance was losing man himself." Gilson is attacking one aspect of what has come to be called **humanism.** The Renaissance humanists (teachers of the humanities – poetry, moral philosophy, and other subjects having to do with man rather than with God or the lower creatures) had no single program, but in their zeal for newly discovered ancient pagan writings and for ancient ideals of liberty, they sometimes stressed secular activity and neglected spiritual subservience to Christ or to the Church. From the ancients some humanists derived a view of man that, by its stress on reason, put in question the traditional view that man was a weak, fallen creature who gained dignity only by submitting to authority. However, many humanists reading pagan works must have asked themselves, with John Lyly, °Elizabethan novelist and playwright, "Is Aristotle more dear to thee with his books than Christ with his blood?" At its most secular, humanism appears in the huffings of Marlowe's Tamburlaine:

> Our souls, whose faculties can comprehend
> The wondrous architecture of the world,
> And measure every wandering planet's course,
> Still climbing after knowledge infinite,
> And always moving as the restless spheres,
> Will us to wear ourselves, and never rest,
> Until we reach the ripest fruit of all,
> That perfect bliss and sole felicity,
> The sweet fruition of an earthly crown.

But humanism in the Renaissance was usually fused with Christianity, and of **Christian humanism** perhaps Erasmus and Milton are the prime examples. When Erasmus said, "Holy Socrates, pray for us," he was seeking to unite the reasonableness of the ancients with the Revelation of Christianity. Milton, too, avoids the excesses of godless humanism. His treatise *Of Education* does not simply define a complete education as "that which fits a man to perform justly, skilfully, and magnanimously all the offices, both private and public, of peace and war," but also says that the aim of learning "is to repair the ruins of our first parents by regaining to know God aright, and out of that knowledge to love him, to imitate him, to be like him, as we may the nearest by possessing our souls of true virtue, which, being united to the heavenly grace of faith, makes up the highest perfection." (Consult W. K. Ferguson, *The Renaissance in Historical Thought*; G. Highet, *The Classical Tradition*; D. Bush, *The Renaissance and English Humanism* and his *Mythology and the Renaissance Tradition in*

English Poetry; and C. S. Lewis, *English Literature in the Sixteenth Century.* On humanism in eighteenth-century England, consult P. Fussell, *The Rhetorical World of Augustan Humanism.*)

repartee. See °comedy.

resolution. See °plot.

Restoration. In 1660 Charles II was restored to the English throne, thus bringing to an end the °Puritan Interregnum, which had abolished the monarchy in 1649. The Restoration Period has no precise end, but is commonly regarded as running to 1700. Taste centered in the Court, which is usually characterized as witty, urbane, and licentious. (For Restoration drama, see °heroic drama [under °tragedy], and °comedy of manners [under °comedy]. Consult G. Sherburn, "The Restoration and Eighteenth Century," in *A Literary History of England,* ed. A. C. Baugh, and also published separately.)

revenge play. See °tragedy.

reversal. See °tragedy and °plot.

rhetoric. The art of using words effectively, or, especially, the art of persuading. Cicero suggested that the orator has three duties – to teach, to persuade, to move – and thus rhetoric overlaps literature. Another view of classical rhetoric sees it as of three sorts: *hortatory,* aiming at persuading to a course of action (especially by reference to the speaker's ethical character); *judicial,* aiming at establishing guilt or innocence (especially by logic); and *ceremonial,* aiming at praising great men (especially by appealing to the hearer's feelings). A pejorative view of rhetoric sees it as skillful lying or as artful empty sentences ("mere rhetoric"). (For definitions of hundreds of terms [mostly Greek] used to name rhetorical figures – *i.e.,* such artful uses of language as °apostrophe, °chiasmus, °onomatopoeia, °paradox, and °zeugma – consult R. A. Lanham, *A Handlist of Rhetorical Terms;* Sister Miriam Joseph, *Shakespeare's Use of the Arts of Language;* and B. Vickers, *Classical Rhetoric in English Poetry.*)

rhyme. See °versification.

rhyme royal. See °versification.

rhythm. See °versification.

rising action. See °plot.

rising meter. See °versification.

ritual. A ceremonial act, an observance or customary procedure. Primitive people perform ritual dances to induce rain, to make crops grow tall, to drive out sickness, etc. Rituals, that is, often attempt to order seemingly chaotic experiences. We have rituals at most critical moments – birth, commencement, marriage, death – marking the importance of these moments and sometimes (as in some prayers for the dead) to induce a desired effect. Much literature seems to have originated in ritual. The precise ritual behind Greek tragedy is uncertain, but it is almost surely descended from some ritual imitating growth and death, or mutability. A common theory holds that it imitates the decline of a vegetation god from spring to winter; the potent tragic hero moves from power to weakness, allegedly a remote descendant of rituals imitating the Year-Spirit who annually died. A ritual inducing the rebirth of the Year-Spirit (spring comes again) is often said to be behind the ancient comic pattern, which moves from threats to joyous feasts and marriages (*i.e.*, to fertility).

Putting aside the debatable question of origins, art, in its public and stereotyped character, is often ritualistic. °Elegies, to take an obvious example, publicly honor men in a more or less traditional way. In addition to being somewhat ritualistic, a good deal of contemporary writing takes for its theme the importance of ritual in daily living. Faulkner's boys who learn the intricacies of hunting and thus are initiated into the group of men and Hemingway's matadors who beautifully kill bulls or his waiters who skillfully pour whisky into glasses impose a neat pattern on the apparent chaos of life by performing rituals and are thus judged worthy.

roman à clef. See °novel.

romance. See °novel.

romantic, romanticism. See °classic and romantic.

rules. See (under °unity) °Three Unities, and also °classic and romantic.

run-on line. See °versification.

saga. Most narrowly, sagas are traditional Icelandic prose tales of about 1000–1200 A.D., orally composed and recited (though later written down), setting forth the heroic deeds and intrigues of families and tempestuous times. More loosely, they are heroic stories or stories covering several generations. (Consult R. Scholes and R. Kellogg, *The Nature of Narrative;* and W. P. Ker, *Epic and Romance.*)

sarcasm. See °irony.

satire. A literary work ridiculing identifiable objects in real life, thus seeking to arouse in the reader contempt for its object. Satirists almost always justify their attacks by claiming that satire is therapeutic, and because they assume that fixed norms exist to which men should adhere, they tend to be °classic rather than romantic. (Many of the notable achievements of the neoclassical period in England, from the later seventeenth century to the later eighteenth, including the work of Butler, Dryden, Pope, Swift, and Burns, are satiric.) Satire is sometimes distinguished from °comedy on the grounds that satire aims to correct by ridiculing, while comedy aims simply to evoke amusement, sometimes even at the speaker's own expense. Pope gave a typical justification of satire when he wrote that nothing "moves strongly but satire, and those who are ashamed of nothing else are so of being ridiculous." Pope also commented that satire "heals with Morals what it hurts with wit." And Swift insisted that the satire he wrote was not malice but medicine:

> His satire points at no defect,
> But what all mortals may correct. . . .
> He spared a hump or crooked nose,
> Whose owners set not up for beaux.

But Swift also saw the futility of satire: "Satire is a sort of glass wherein beholders do generally discover everybody's face but their own."

At its simplest, satire can be **invective** – strong denunciation – which touches on satire when it couples its verbal abuse with entertainment, when it displays °wit as well as passion. Here is a borderline sample from *King Lear:*

> *Kent*. Fellow, I know thee.
> *Oswald*. What dost thou know me for?
> *Kent*. A knave, a rascal, an eater of broken meats; a base, proud, shallow, beggarly, three-suited, hundred-pound, filthy worsted-stocking knave; a lily-livered, action-taking knave; a whoreson, glass-gazing, super-serviceable, finical rogue; one-truck-inheriting slave; one that wouldst be a bawd in way of good service, and art nothing but the composition of a knave, beggar, coward, pandar, and the son and heir of a mongrel bitch.

Such a scurrilous personal attack, in verse or prose, is also called a **lampoon.** Satire ranges from such bludgeonings to °burlesque where the object of contempt is almost lost sight of amid the satirist's fanciful creation, as in parts of *Alice's Adventures in Wonderland*. The great bulk of important satires are somewhere in between these extremes, employing °irony, as Dryden said in his *Origin . . . of Satire* (1693), in order to "make a man appear a fool, a blockhead, or a knave without using any of those opprobrious terms!" Pope, in "The Rape of the Lock," by ironically bestowing °epic grandeur on a trivial quarrel, deflates it:

> Then flashed the living fire from her eyes,
> And screams of horror rend th'affrighted skies.
> Not louder shrieks to pitying Heaven are cast,
> When husbands, or when lapdogs breathe their last.

Two Roman poets, Horace (65–8 B.C.) and Juvenal (55–130 A.D.), have given their names to two kinds of satire: **Horatian satire** genially attacks foibles and follies; **Juvenalian satire** passionately attacks vices and crimes. Dryden summarizes the difference: "Horace is always on the amble, Juvenal on the gallop." Northrop Frye has recently emphasized another sort, **Menippean satire,** characterized by its form rather than by its tone. The work of Menippus (fl. 290 B.C.) is lost, but that of his successors survives. Frye suggests in his *Anatomy of Criticism* that Menippean satire "deals less with people . . . than with mental attitudes," and he places Swift's *Gulliver* in this category, along with work by Petronius, Rabelais, Voltaire, Thomas Love Peacock, Lewis Carroll, and Aldous Huxley. (This has the virtue of seeing these works of prose fiction as something other than novels with poor characterization and poor plots.) Menippean satire – a term Frye suggests might be replaced by "the **anatomy**" – usually ridicules the pretentious wise man (pedant, philosopher, scientist), presenting its characters not realistically but as mouthpieces for erudite ideas which by their very erudition make themselves absurd. Short Menippean satires are often dialogues, longer ones resemble loosely knit novels and usually manage to bring the talkers together at a banquet or country house where they anatomize ideas and overwhelm each other and themselves with erudition.

Satire is sometimes divided into **indirect satire** and **formal satire.** The author of indirect satire (*e.g.*, a Menippean satire) presents a fantastic story, however slight, with invented characters. But in a formal satire there is no story; the only speaker is the author who, in his own person, attacks in colloquial language the immorality and folly that he sees around him. Byron writes formal satire when he says:

> Prepare for rhyme – I'll publish, right or wrong:
> Fools are my theme, let satire be my song.

Ezra Pound (in *Literary Essays*) puts his finger on what Horatian, Juvenalian, Menippean, and all other satire have in common: "Satire reminds one that certain things are not worth while. It draws one to consider time wasted." (See °burlesque and °comedy. Consult, in addition to Frye, J. Sutherland, *English Satire;* G. Highet, *The Classical Tradition;* M. Mack, "The Muse of Satire," *The Yale Review,* 41 [1951], 80–92; R. C. Elliott, *The Power of Satire;* R. Paulson, *The Fictions of Satire;* and A. Kernan, *The Plot of Satire.*)

scansion. See °versification.

scene. See °act.

science fiction. Narrative (ranging from °short stories to long °novels) that customarily takes a scientific or pseudo-scientific hypothesis and then gives us a vision of what life would be like if the hypothesis were true. Though seemingly fanciful, in its detailed facts or presumptive facts and in its adherence to its hypothesis, it is opposed to fantasy worlds of capricious magical creatures. It often includes grim satire on life as we know it: bureaucrats are petty and inefficient, military men are ruthless, machines tyrannize, human beings are dehumanized. (Consult K. Amis, *New Maps of Hell.*)

scop. See °bard.

sensibility. See °sentimental and, for another use, °dissociation of sensibility.

sententia. See °aphorism.

sentimental. Generally a pejorative word in literary criticism, indicating a superabundance of tender emotion, a disproportionate amount of sentiment (feeling). Seymour, in J. D. Salinger's "Raise High the Roof Beam, Carpenter," defines sentimentality as giving "to a thing more tenderness than God gives to it." It is sentimental to be intensely distressed because one has stepped on a flower. A character, say, Hamlet, may display deep emotions, but they are sentimental only if they are in excess of what we feel the situation warrants. (Consult L. Lerner, *The Truest Poetry.*) More specifically, "sentimental" writing refers to writing wherein evil is denied or overlooked or bathed in a glow of forgiving tenderness. In the eighteenth century the ability to respond emotionally (usually tearfully) to acts of benevolence or malevolence – in short, to abound in emotional morality – was called **sensibility.** Late in the century Wordsworth (then age sixteen) wrote a poem, "On Seeing Miss Helen Maria Williams Weep at a Tale of Distress":

> She wept. — Life's purple tide began to flow
> In languid streams through every thrilling vein;
> Dim were my swimming eyes — my pulse beat slow,
> And my full heart was swelled to dear delicious pain.

Thus, in the **literature of sensibility,** such as the **sentimental novel** (*e.g.*, Mackenzie's *The Man of Feeling*) and the **sentimental drama** (*e.g.*, Cibber's *Love's Last Shift*), there is at the expense of reason an emphasis on tearful situations; man's benevolent emotions are overestimated, for he is assumed to be innately good, and villains reform, usually in bursts of repenting tears. There is little °wit (see °comedy), the characters are usually of the middle class, and they demonstrate their virtue by weeping at the sight of distress. In his "Comparison between Sentimental and Laughing Comedy" (1773), Oliver Goldsmith attacked **sentimental comedy,** saying that in it

> . . . the virtues of private life are exhibited, rather than the vices exposed; and the distresses rather than the faults of mankind make our interest in the piece. . . . Almost all the characters are good, . . . and though they want humor, have abundance of sentiment and feeling. If they happen to have faults or foibles, the spectator is taught not only to pardon, but to applaud them, in consideration of the goodness of their hearts; so that folly, instead of being ridiculed, is commended, and the comedy aims at touching our passions, without the power of being truly pathetic.

Northrop Frye, in *Fables of Identity*, offers a higher view of some late eighteenth-century writers (notably Smart and Blake), suggesting that in "an age of sensibility" literature is conceived of as a process rather than as a finished product; it is often oracular, a fragmentary utterance by a poet in a trance-like state where ideas are freely associated and where sound (*e.g.*, °alliteration and °refrain) is used almost for its own sake. (Consult E. Bernbaum, *The Drama of Sensibility;* A. Sherbo, *English Sentimental Drama;* and L. I. Bredvold, *The Natural History of Sensibility*. For another use of "sensibility," see °dissociation of sensibility.)

septenary. See °versification.

sequence. A group of related scenes in a film. Within a sequence there may be an **intercut,** a switch to another action that, for example, provides an ironic comment on the main action of the sequence. If intercuts are so abundant in a sequence that, in effect, two or more sequences are going at once (*e.g.*, °shots of the villain about to ravish the heroine alternating with shots of the hero riding to her rescue), we have a **cross-cut.** In the example just given, probably the tempo would increase, the shots becoming progressively shorter as we get to the rescue. (See °cuts.)

sestet. See °versification.

setting. See °atmosphere.

shaped poetry. Poems whose lines, when printed, form a picture. George Herbert's "The Altar" is an example:

A broken ALTAR, Lord, thy servant rears,
Made of a heart, and cemented with tears:
Whose parts are as thy hand did frame;
No workman's tool hath touched the same.
A HEART alone
Is such a stone,
As nothing but
Thy power doth cut.
Wherefore each part
Of my hard heart
Meets in this frame,
To praise thy Name:
That, if I chance to hold my peace,
These stones to praise thee may not cease.
Oh let thy blessed SACRIFICE be mine,
And sanctify this ALTAR to be thine.

(Consult C. C. Bombaugh, *Oddities and Curiosities,* pp. 92–97, 350. For modern examples, consult John Hollander, *Types of Shape*.)

short story. Narrative prose fiction shorter than the °novel, usually not more than 15,000 words. It is impossible to distinguish a short story from a novel on any single basis other than length, and there is no established length for either. "Long story" and "short novel" are pigeonholes for works that, because of their length, do not seem classifiable as short stories or novels. One cannot say that a short story has more °unity than a novel, for both may be equally unified – just as a °sonnet and an °epic may be equally unified, though the latter is far longer. Nor can one say that a short story deals with fewer characters, or with a briefer period of time than does a novel, for while this is frequently so, a story of a few pages may mention numerous characters and cover decades, while a long novel may limit itself to a single day in the lives of three or four persons. Since a good short story and a good novel make the most of their length, one can perhaps say that the good novel is necessarily more complex than the good short story. Most frequently a short-story writer of the nineteenth or twentieth centuries focuses on a single character in a single episode, and, rather than tracing his development, reveals him at a particular moment. As Poe put it, in reviewing Hawthorne's *Twice-Told Tales,* the writer of a story conceives of "a certain unique or single effect to be brought out." (Older stories such as *The Arabian Nights* and Boccaccio's *Decameron* often put less emphasis on character revelation and more on ingenious happenings.) But the novelist usually does more – perhaps he handles more characters, perhaps covers in detail a greater period of time, perhaps covers more aspects of his characters, or (to combine the last two points), covers the long-range development of many-sided figures. In some usage, a narrative that decidedly emphasizes happenings rather than character is a **tale** rather than a story or novel. This usage is clearly seen in Lamb's *Tales from Shakespeare* (well-told summaries of what happens in the plays). Furthermore, "tale" often connotes a "yarn," a narrative told simply but about strange happenings, often legendary – a sort of miniature romance rather than a miniature novel. (See °novel.) A ***Märchen*** (German: little tale) is a prose tale passed on by oral transmission, such as the fairy tales collected by the brothers Grimm. *Märchen* is also applied to literary works (especially by such German romantic writers as Novalis and Tieck), longish stories that evoke the mysterious or the supernatural, though such literary tales are more often called *Kunstmärchen* and are thus distinguished from folk tales or *Volksmärchen.* (See °plot and °point of view. Consult S. O'Faolain, *The Short Story,* and his anthology, *Short Stories;* also, four symposia printed in *The Kenyon Review* 1969 and 1970, and reprinted as *The Short Story Today,* ed. G. Lanning and E. White.)

shot. What is recorded between the time a camera starts and the time it stops, *i.e.*, between the director's call for "Action" and his call to "Cut." Rarely a fraction of a second, and usually not longer than fifteen or so seconds, perhaps the average shot is about ten seconds. Three common shots are (1) a **long shot** or **establishing shot,** showing the main object at a considerable distance from the camera and thus presenting it in relation to its general surroundings (*e.g.*, captured soldiers, seen across a prison yard, entering the yard); (2) a **medium shot,** showing the object in relation to its immediate surroundings (*e.g.*, a couple of soldiers, from the knees up, with the yard's wall behind them); (3) a **close-up,** showing only the main object, or, more often, only a part of it (*e.g.*, a soldier's face, or his bleeding feet).

While taking a shot, the camera can move: it can swing to the right or left while its base remains fixed (a **pan shot**), up or down while fixed on its axis (a **tilt shot**), forward or backward (a

traveling shot, or a **tracking shot**), or in and out and up and down fastened to a crane (a **crane shot**). A **zoom shot** uses a zoom lens, which enables the camera to change its focus fluidly, so it can approach a detail – as a traveling shot can – while remaining fixed in place. In Rossellini's *Umberto D*, the desperate old man looks out of the window, and, by means of a zoom shot, the pavement suddenly seems to rush up at the spectator, conveying the idea that the old man is thinking of throwing himself out of the window. A **zoom freeze** brings the action from far away to close-up, and then halts or "freezes" the action by printing additional identical frames. Truffaut's *The 400 Blows* ends with a zoom freeze of the frustrated boy at the edge of the sea; frozen, he apparently neither kills himself nor really continues to live.

Much depends on the angle (high or low) from which the shots are made. If the camera is high (a **high angle shot**), looking down on people, it will dwarf them, perhaps even reduce them to crawling insects, making them pitiful or contemptible. If the camera is low (a **low angle shot**), close to the ground and looking up, thereby showing people against the sky, it probably will give them added dignity. But these are not invariable principles. A low angle shot, for example, does not always add dignity: films in which children play important parts often have lots of low angle shots, showing adults as menacing giants. (Consult R. Huss and N. Silverstein, *The Film Experience;* and R. Stephenson and J. R. Debrix, *The Cinema as Art*.)

simile. See °figurative language.

slapstick. See °comedy.

slice of life. See °naturalism.

slow film. See °film.

soft focus. Deliberately faulty focusing of the camera's lens in order to blur the images or soften lines, common in sentimental and religious films, and in scenes of fainting, delirium, and fantasy. Commonly it introduces a flash-back (an episode earlier than the one just presented). Sometimes only part of the image (*e.g.*, the foreground) is in soft focus, the remainder thus being heightened by contrast.

soliloquy. A speech, most often in °drama, wherein a °character speaks his thoughts aloud while alone. An **aside** is a speech wherein a character expresses his thoughts in words audible to the spectators but supposedly not to the other stage characters present. Both were important °conventions in °Elizabethan drama and, later, in °melodrama, but the late nineteenth century aimed so vigorously to present on the stage the illusion of real life that they were banished. They have, however, been revived in the twentieth century. In Eugene O'Neill's *Strange Interlude,* the asides represent the characters' thoughts and unspoken desires. Both the soliloquy and the aside are **monologues,** but more often "monologue" denotes an extended speech (in a °narrative as well as in a drama) delivered by one character, heard but uninterrupted by others in his presence. (See °stream of consciousness [under °novel], °dramatic monologue, and °convention.)

sonnet. See °versification.

source. See °analogue.

Spenserian stanza. See °versification.

spondee (adjective: **spondiac**). See °versification.

sprung rhythm. See °versification.

stanza. See °versification.

stichomythia. See °dialogue.

still. See °frame.

stock character. See °convention.

stock epithet. See °epic.

stock response. A reader's stereotyped reaction to some stimulus in the work of art, akin to a driver's reaction to a red light. Stock responses in some cases (driving a car) are important, but in literature they may interfere with (block out) a more valuable or appropriate response which the work ought to evoke. If the reader assumes that a °sonnet (see under °versification) can only express love, he will distort and/or reject many nonamorous sonnets. (Consult I. A. Richards, *Practical Criticism.*)

stock situation. See °convention.

story. See °plot and °short story.

straight cut. See °cut.

stream of consciousness novel. See °novel.

stress. See °versification.

strophe. See °ode.

structure. See °form.

style. Refers to the mode of expression, the devices an author employs in his writing. Thus °diction, grammatical constructions, °figurative language, °alliteration and other sound patterns (see °versification) enter into style. I. A. Richards suggests, in *Practical Criticism*, that "many of the secrets of 'style' could . . . be shown to be matters of °tone, of the perfect recognition of the writer's relation to the reader in view of what is being said and their joint feelings about it." Milton's style is not Shakespeare's, and Shakespeare's early style (with many rhymes, for example) is not his late style (with very few rhymes). Most broadly, "style" includes everything – the choice of plots and themes as well as of words and rhythms. Cardinal Newman put it thus: "Thought and meaning are inseparable from each other. Matter and expression are parts of one: style is a thinking out into language."

Styles are often named for authors (Miltonic), books (Biblical), ages (°Renaissance), and subjects (legal). At one extreme are ornate styles, notably the **Isocratic** (for Isocrates, 436–338 B.C.) and the **Euphuistic** (for *Euphues*, a prose fiction by John Lyly, 1554?–1606). In each of these ornate or Asiatic styles there is elaborate balance: clauses often have equal length, equal sounds (°alliteration, etc.), parallel grammatical structure, and parallel or antithetical thoughts. The euphuistic style adds to this structure a good deal of ornament, especially mythology, proverbial lore, and farfetched zoology. Here is a sample of Lyly's euphuism: "But as the chameleon though he have most guts draweth least breath, or as the elder tree though he be fullest of pith is farthest from strength, so though your reasons seem inwardly to yourself somewhat substantial, and your persuasions pithy in your own conceit, yet being well weighed without, they be shadows without substance, and weak without force." The **Ciceronian sentence** (named for Cicero, 106–43 B.C.) is also fairly long, assured, and dignified, usually balanced or antithetical, but it sounds less mechanical than the Isocratic or Euphuistic sentence, and it flows out to a crescendo. It is usually **periodic,** that is, its clauses are not independent, and thus suspense is created because the meaning is suspended until the end. "Of lyrics, odes, elegies, and epics, I will say nothing" is – though unusually brief – periodic, because there is balance and because the meaning is not clear until the last word is said. Here is a Ciceronian sentence, from Dr. Johnson's *Life of Dryden:* "To search his plays for vigorous sallies and sententious elegances, or to fix the dates of any little pieces which he wrote by chance or by solicitation, were labor too tedious and minute."

In England in the late sixteenth century there was a reaction against Ciceronian prose, and the **baroque** or **loose sentence** gained favor. The baroque sentence is anti-Ciceronian, for it does not use parallel constructions and move to a climax. Whereas the Ciceronian period, by holding the full meaning suspended until the climactic end, suggests an assured speaker who from the first knows where he is going, the baroque sentence, by stating the main idea first, and then adding modifications and parenthetical thoughts in unparallel clauses, suggests a speaker in the process of improvising his thought. A baroque sentence usually has several independent clauses, linked by colons and semicolons, or by such simple co-ordinates as "and" and "or." This sample is from John Donne: "We study health, and we deliberate upon our meats and drink and air and exercises, and we hew and we polish every stone that goes to that building; and so our health is a long and regular work." Notice that "baroque," applied to sentences, connotes something rather different from "baroque" as applied to architecture, for baroque architecture often is elaborately symmetrical. The baroque style is sometimes subdivided into the Attic and the Senecan styles. An **Attic sentence** (named for Attica, a Greek province) suggests, for some critics, a gentleman's talk: clear, concentrated, simple. It does not often balance clauses exactly against each other. Here is an example from Addison: "There is no character more frequently given to a writer than that of being a 'genius.' I have heard many a little sonneteer called a fine genius." But this illustration is from the eighteenth century. The earlier anti-Ciceronian or Attic writing is rarely so cool. More often it uses a **Senecan sentence**, which is commonly pointed, *i.e.*, aphoristic, and in some degree balanced in sound and sense with antitheses, but not as elaborate or as decorated as a Euphuistic sentence or as periodic as a Ciceronian sentence. The overall effect is of curtness and asymmetry, as the following quotation (1573) suggests: "As for Ciceronians and sugar-tongued fellows, which labor more for fineness of speech than for knowledge of good matter, they oft speak much to small purpose, and shaking forth a number of choice words and picked sentences, they hinder good learning with their fond chat." (For a discussion and recommended readings consult J. Barish, "Baroque Prose," *Publications of the Modern Language Association*, 73 [1958], 185–95, and two books by M. Croll, *"Attic" and Baroque Prose Style*, and *Style, Rhetoric and Rhythm*. See also °baroque.)

An overused stylistic device, such as *Time* magazine's °epithets, is called a **mannerism;** on a single page of *Time* one finds "Icy-blooded sometime Playboy Luis Miguel Dominguín," "boyish Antonio Ordoñez," "U.S. Supreme Court Justice Thomas

Clark," "TV-Radio Impressario Arthur Godfrey," "New York's Governor Nelson Rockefeller," and "world-topping, bee-keeping Sir Edmund Hillary."

Jonathan Swift defined good style as "proper words in proper places"; the choice of the proper word is a matter of **decorum.** George Puttenham, who in *The Art of English Poesie* (1589) defined decorum as "a lovely conformity," objects to a translation of Vergil which says Aeneas trudged out of Troy, for "trudge" is (he says) inappropriate to noble persons. On the other hand, rough, varied °meters would be decorous (appropriate) for a king who lived discordantly. Words unsuited for some poems may thus be suited for others. For example, because °satire often belittles ignoble behavior, vulgar words are acceptable there that are inappropriate in an °epic on the lofty work of the founding of Rome.

Style is sometimes divided into three sorts: **high** (or **grand**) **style, middle style,** and **low** (or **plain**) **style.** A style is decorous when it is appropriate to the speaker, the audience, the subject, and the occasion. Thus, the grand style presupposes importance all around, *e.g.*, Churchill addressing England just after the evacuation at Dunkirk. (On the problem of style as ornament vs. style as a part of meaning, see °form. Consult F. L. Lucas, *Style;* J. A. K. Thomson, *The Classical Background of English Literature*, and his *Classical Influences on English Prose; Style in Prose Fiction*, ed. H. C. Martin; *Essays on the Language of Literature*, ed. S. Chatman and S. R. Levin, and *The Problem of Style*, ed. J. V. Cunningham.)

subjective and **objective.** The subjective writer is said to create art out of aspects of his own personality. He may draw heavily on his own experiences for subject-matter, or, if writing about episodes that were not lived by him, he may assert his personality by commenting on them. In any case, the reader of a subjective work feels that he has some knowledge of the author's life or views. Wordsworth's *Prelude* is subjective because, as he himself said, it records "the origin and progress of his own powers." In a narrower sense, subjective is limited to a work that is the product of so highly idiosyncratic a personality that it is intelligible only to the initiate. An **objective** writer is one who annihilates his own personality and whose art reveals little or nothing of himself. In Shakespeare there are varied comments about marriage, yet few critics today would hold that these comments reveal anything about Shakespeare's own marriage or about his attitude toward that institution. Notice, too, that Shakespeare's sonnets may be similarly objective, for though they talk of "I," the "I" may be a fictional dramatic creation or °persona (mask) expressing an emotion, and not the poet himself. Thus an author's characters may speak of themselves and express their emotions fully, but the author is subjective only if the ideas and emotions expressed are his own. (For Keats on objectivity [or "°negative capability," as he called it], see his letter of October 27, 1818. On subjective literary criticism, see °criticism. For a history of the terms, consult M. H. Abrams, *The Mirror and the Lamp*, Ch. 9.)

summary. See °plot.

surprise. See °suspense.

surrealism. The successor to °Dadaism, surrealism was a movement, especially vigorous in France in the 1920's and 1930's, that sought to go beyond the domain usually considered "real," into the "super-real," which includes the world of the unconscious – the world, for example, of dreams. Surrealists are especially hostile to rationality, middle-class ideals, and artistic °conventions, holding that all these shape – and deform – the creations of the unconscious. Sir Herbert Read, an advocate of the movement, describes a dream that he versified when he awoke. Commenting on the poem, he explains that "there are several rhymes, but no regular rhyme system; these rhymes were not sought by me, but came unconsciously in the act of writing the poem. If I had sought for rhymes I should inevitably have been compelled to distort my narrative and my °imagery, and to that extent to be false to my inspiration" (*The Philosophy of Modern Art*). Surrealism, in its emphasis on spontaneity, feeling, and sincerity, is obviously related to °romanticism. Wallace Stevens, in *Opus Posthumous*, complained that surrealism "invents without discovering," revealing not the unconscious but merely the familiar "plus imagination," such as a clam playing the accordian. (Consult M. A. Caws, *The Poetry of Dada and Sur-realism*.)

suspense. Uncertainty, often characterized by anxiety. Suspense is usually a curious mixture of pain and pleasure, as Gwendolen, in Oscar Wilde's *The Importance of Being Earnest*, implies: "The suspense is terrible. I hope it will last." Most great art relies more heavily on suspense than on **surprise.** One can rarely reread works depending on surprise; the surprise gone, the interest is gone. Suspense is usually achieved in part by **foreshadowing** – hints of what is to come. As Coleridge said, Shakespeare gives us not surprise but expectation and then the satisfaction of perfect knowledge: "As the feeling with which we startle at a shooting star, compared with that of watching the sunrise at the pre-established moment, such and so low is surprise compared with expectation." Shakespeare, in fact, like the Greek dramatists, often used well-known stories, and though the audience presumably was not surprised by the deaths of Caesar and Brutus, it enjoyed the suspense of anticipating them. Suspense is thus related to tragic °irony. The tragic character moves closer and closer to his doom, and though he may be surprised by it, we are not; we are held by suspense. If, in fact, he is suddenly and unexpectedly saved (as is a hero of a °melodrama), we may feel cheated.

symbolism. Derived from Greek *symballein*, "to throw together," which thus suggests the essential quality of symbolism: the drawing together of two worlds, the revelation of an otherwise invisible world through the presentation of the concrete material world of roses, toads, caves, stars, etc. As a noun, the original Greek word denoted half of something broken in two, and thus the word suggests not something that stands for something else, but something that is part of a larger unit. The symbol is often distinguished from the **sign,** which is merely a shorthand device, standing for something else: a green light is a sign for "Go," and × is a mathematician's sign for "multiply." These signs do not reveal anything otherwise inexpressible, nor are they part of a whole. A blue light, or a "beep," or the smell of peppermint could equally well stand for "Go." But the symbol of, say, the sacrificed lamb may (for the Christian who holds that concrete phenomena are manifestations of another world) reveal aspects of Christ otherwise inexpressible.

Symbolism is also distinguished from °allegory. Whereas the allegorist commonly invents a world (Bunyan's man named Christian, in *The Pilgrim's Progress*, meets a Giant named Despair) in order to talk about the real world, the symbolist commonly presents the phenomena of what we usually call the real world, and he uses them to reveal a "higher," eternal world of which the symbol is a part. In allegory there is a system of equations, but in symbolism there is an extension. The allegorist is free to invent any number of imaginary worlds to talk about the real world, but the symbolist feels that there is only one way by which he can present the "higher" real world he envisions. The everyday world is thus often considered by symbolists as a concrete but transient version of a more important realm, and the symbolist who presents, say, a rose, is (he might hold) speaking about a rose and also about the eternal beauty of womanhood in the only possible way. The allegorist, who can invent half a dozen ways of embodying his idea, does not insist on the reality of his invented world. An allegory can with relative ease be °paraphrased, but a symbol, because it not only stands for something else which cannot otherwise be expressed, but also is *part of something else* and *is itself too*, cannot be clearly explained. As Carlyle says in *Sartor Resartus*, in a symbol "the Infinite is made to blend itself with the Finite, to stand visible, and as it were, attainable there." Henry James says that symbolism is the presentation "of objects casting . . . far behind them a shadow more curious . . . than the apparent figure." Having said all this, it must be mentioned that there is an increasing tendency to blur the distinction between symbol and allegory, especially when the writer's invented world (usually associated with allegory) has no clear equations.

The symbol (which may be a situation, character, or scene in a work – *e.g.*, birth, an infant, or a manger) is given unusual stress, perhaps by repetition within the literary work, or from one of the author's works to another, and so it is highly potent, richly suggestive. This stress, this dwelling on the thing distinguishes the symbol from the °metaphor (see °figurative language). The user of the metaphor says, "My love is a red rose" or "My rose," but he is writing about his love; the symbolist says "My rose" and is writing about a rose – a rose which stirs a train of thought about something else, too, and which is thus a rose and something more than a mere rose. A **natural symbol** inherently resembles the higher thing which it suggests and of which it is a part: the rose is inherently beautiful; the sun (though sometimes destructive) is inherently the nurturer of life. These symbols appear widely in literature even of separated cultures. A **private symbol** is one not commonly accepted, but unique to the user: for W. B. Yeats, the heron symbolizes subjectivity. If a private symbol becomes widely accepted, and is used by other writers, it becomes a **conventional symbol.** The conventional symbol (such as the nightingale, often associated with melancholy), even though it is recognized only through agreement, is not a sign (like the traffic light) because, again, it presumably arouses deep feelings and is regarded as possessing properties beyond what the eye alone sees.

Even if one rejects the symbolist's common idea of a "higher" world, one can still hold that symbols exert an appeal – especially to the unconscious depths of the mind – which arbitrarily invented allegory does not. Jungian psychology, for example, holds that repeated experiences of the human race (*e.g.*, birth) are suggested in °images and °motifs that recur in °myth and literature (*e.g.*, a journey out of a dark place). These recurrent themes, or °archetypes, as Jung calls them, evoke a response from the unconscious that cannot be otherwise evoked. (See °myth.) Whether or not Jung's postulated "collective unconscious" with its store of archetypal memories exists, readers do respond deeply to the presentation in literature of certain images and motifs. Such images and motifs, stimulating the percipient to regard them as something more than they seem to be in themselves, are commonly called symbols. It is sometimes difficult, of course, to decide whether, say, a hanged man in a story is a symbol of Christ, or is simply a hanged man. But if he stirs in us strong thoughts of Christ, and we in some degree regard him as Christ and feel that we come to some deeper understanding of Christ, modern usage allows us to call him a symbol of Christ.

Symbolism is probably as old as literature, but in the second half of the nineteenth century there arose, first in France, the so-called **Symbolist Movement** (notice the capitals), which included notably Mallarmé and Valéry. Some Symbolists, like earlier symbolic writers, presupposed an invisible world beyond that of concrete phenomena. W. B. Yeats, influenced by French Symbolists, said that an artistic work is like a magic talisman: "it entangles . . . a part of the Divine essence." But other Symbolists found the concrete world merely a stimulus to their minds. For these latter, a rose, say, was neither a real thing nor an embodiment of a divine essence; it merely evoked emotions, which were communicated by words whose sounds allegedly evoked the same emotions in the reader. The extreme Symbolists held with Mallarmé that poetry was sound with associations rather than words with meaning.

(For symbolism in general, consult H. Levin, *Contexts of Criticism;* I. Hungerland, *Poetic Discourse;* R. May, *Symbolism in Religion and Literature;* and E. Fromm, *The Forgotten Language.* For the Symbolist Movement, consult C. M. Bowra, *The Heritage of Symbolism;* E. Wilson, *Axel's Castle;* and A. Balakian, *The Symbolist Movement.*)

sympathy. See °empathy and °pathos.

synecdoche. See °figurative language.

synesthesia. See °figurative language.

tale. See °short story.

tenor. See °figurative language.

tension. See °form.

tercet. See °versification.

terza rima. See °versification.

tetrameter. See °versification.

texture. See °form.

theme. See °plot.

Three Unities. See °unity.

threnody. See °elegy.

tilt shot. See °shot.

tone. The attitude of the author, as the reader infers it, in the work. Just as a speaker's tone of voice may indicate an attitude toward his subject and his hearer of, say, scorn or delight or solemnity, so an author's tone is his attitude. Tone should not be confused with °atmosphere, which is the world in which the characters move. The atmosphere of a work may be frightful, but the tone may be compassionate or bewildered. Atmosphere may be complicated by tone. Jonathan Swift's "A Modest Proposal for Preventing the Children of Poor People in Ireland from Being a Burden to Their Parents or Country" is an °essay ostensibly written by a sincere economist who has evolved a humane plan. The atmosphere — as the title indicates — is one of earnestness. But as the speaker continues and explains matter-of-factly that this commendable goal is to be achieved by eating the children, the reader perceives that Swift is largely °satirizing economic programs that neglect human values. The economist keeps talking, presenting his statistics, but his self-assured earnestness is not the author's tone, the author's attitude as we come to infer it. (See °style.)

topic (or ***topos;*** plural: ***topoi***). For Aristotle, both the material out of which an argument is made and the form of the argument; a rhetorical commonplace or set-piece, such as the comparison of a man's face to a book, or the epic poet's assertion that he undertakes "things unattempted yet in prose or rhyme." (On these topics, consult E. R. Curtius, *European Literature and the Latin Middle Ages*.) The term has been extended to mean something like a °motif, *e.g.*, a description of an ideal landscape, or the Seven Ages of Man, or the °Golden Age.

tracking shot. See °shot.

tragedy. For Aristotle, tragedy was a dramatic °imitation (representation) of an "°action of high importance." For us, it is generally a play ending with death or (especially in the °naturalistic tragedies since the latter part of the nineteenth century) ending with the hero alive but spiritually crushed. Aristotle attributes ***hamartia*** to the tragic hero. This Greek word is variously translated as "tragic flaw" or "error" or "shortcoming" or "weakness," and in many plays it *is* a flaw or even a vice such as ***hybris*** (also ***hubris***) – Greek for overweening pride, arrogance, excessive confidence. But in other plays it is merely a misstep, such as a choice that turns out badly. A somewhat more favorable view sees *hybris* as the hero's attempt to express the full dimensions of human vitality – an attempt which violates the laws of order, for the hero seeks to introduce absolute perfection in a world that is merely relative. Indeed, the tragic hero is sometimes undone by his virtue – his courage, for example, when others are not merely prudent but cowardly. It may, therefore, be a serious misconception to insist that a tragic hero necessarily has a moral fault (*e.g.*, to attribute lust or rashness to Romeo and Juliet). (On *hamartia* and *hybris* see R. Lattimore, *Story Patterns in Greek Tragedy*, Ch. 2.)

In any case, the hero suffers, whether for a moral weakness, an error, or a virtue. After suffering, he usually comes to some sort of awareness, either of his vice, if he had one, or of his own virtue, which he now sees cannot exist in a world of ordinary men. This recognition (a mental and/or a moral enlargement) is sometimes said to minimize the hero's pain and the audience's pity and fear; it is also sometimes said to be precisely the tragic quality. That is, tragedy dramatizes (it may be held) the fact that men can only see clearly when they have been subjected to such great pressures that they are destroyed in the process. Aristotle (and countless followers) said that tragedy evokes pity and fear, and that it produces in the spectator a **catharsis** (purgation, or, some scholars hold, purification) of these emotions: it drains or perhaps refines these emotions, and thus tragedy is socially useful. (Aristotle's *Poetics*, a fragmentary discussion of literature, is the subject of much controversy; one cannot with security assert that Aristotle said anything without a counterargument being offered. For various views of catharsis, consult Lucas, cited below, and G. F. Else's monumental *Aristotle's Poetics*.)

Two other words ought to be mentioned here: Aristotle's ***peripeteia*** (Anglicized to **peripety**, meaning **reversal**) and his ***anagnorisis*** (meaning **disclosure, discovery**, or **recognition**). The former occurs when an action produces the opposite of what was intended or expected, and it is therefore a kind of °irony. For example, Macbeth kills Duncan to gain happiness but reaps misery instead. For Aristotle the "recognition" or "disclosure" seems to be merely a recognition of who is who, by such tokens as birthmarks, clothes, etc., but the term has been usefully extended to include the tragic hero's recognition of himself and/or of the essence of life. Thus, Othello, having murdered his faithful wife, learns he was beguiled into thinking her dishonest, and finally recognizes himself as "one not easily jealous, but being wrought / Perplexed in the extreme"; and he exacts justice from himself by suicide.

A **Senecan tragedy** is a serious play by the Roman author Seneca (4 B.C.–65 A.D.), or an imitation of such a play. Of the ten extant Roman tragedies, nine are attributed to Seneca, and these were probably written not for the stage but for private readings. The heroes seem to us to be almost madmen, but perhaps they are to be regarded sympathetically as people overwhelmed by passion. Seneca's influence on the Elizabethan dramatists was considerable; the **revenge play**, with its ghosts and its deranged hero who seeks vengeance, doubtless would have been different had Seneca not existed. Among the signs of Seneca's influence are: ghosts, revenge, deeds of horror (*e.g.*, children stewed and served to their parents), occasional stoical speeches but a predominance of passionate speeches, use of °stichomythia (see °dialogue), and a ***nuntius*** (messenger) who recites in a heightened style an off-stage happening (*e.g.*, the wounded soldier in *Macbeth*, I.i). But, of course, not every use of any of these characteristics is necessarily attributable to Seneca's influence. And there are differences: the horrors in Seneca are narrated, but in *King Lear* Gloucester is blinded on the stage. (Consult F. L. Lucas, *Seneca and Elizabethan Tragedy*; M. Doran, *Endeavors of Art*; W. Farnham, *The Medieval Heritage of Elizabethan Tragedy*; and F. Bowers, *Elizabethan Revenge Tragedy 1587–1642*. H. Baker, *Induction to Tragedy*, minimizes Seneca's influence.)

From the Greeks until the seventeenth century, tragedy almost always dealt with persons of high rank; but with the rise of the middle class, °bourgeois or domestic tragedy developed. There are a few °Elizabethan examples of plays with a middle-class hero and many eighteenth-century ones (often °sentimental). Arthur Miller's *Death of a Salesman* is a modern example. By contrast, **heroic tragedy,** popular in England during the °Restoration Period (1660–1700), presented high-ranking characters who, larger than life, felt and °bombastically expressed enormous passions and accomplished enormous deeds. The subject of heroic tragedy – or more generally, **heroic drama,** for it often ends untragically – is commonly the clash between love and honor, with empires at stake.

(Consult F. L. Lucas, *Tragedy* [2nd ed.]; T. R. Henn, *The Harvest of Tragedy*; H. J. Muller, *The Spirit of Tragedy*; M. Prior, *The Language of Tragedy*; and R. Sewall, *The Vision of Tragedy*. See also °plot, °tragicomedy, °suspense, °comic relief, °pathos.)

tragicomedy. °Renaissance critical theorists assumed that °tragedies dealt with noble (important) figures and ended with a death; °comedies dealt with trivial (laughable) figures and ended with a celebration. A tragicomedy was some sort of mixture: high characters in a play ending happily, or a mingling of deaths and feasts, or, most often (as in many American films) threats of death which are happily evaded. John Fletcher (1579–1625), who with his collaborator Francis Beaumont wrote graceful °dramas relying heavily on passionate outbursts and surprising turns of °plot, defined a tragicomedy as a play that lacks deaths (and thus is no tragedy) but "brings some near it, which is enough to make it no comedy." (Consult E. Waith, *The Pattern of Tragi-Comedy;* and K. S. Guthke, *Modern Tragi-Comedy.*)

tranche de vie. See °naturalism.

transferred epithet. See °figurative language.

traveling shot. See °shot.

travesty. See °burlesque.

trimeter. See °versification.

triplet. See °versification.

trochee (adjective: **trochaic**). See °versification.

trope. See °figurative language.

type (***tupos***) or **figure** (***figura***). In Biblical criticism, an Old Testament person, thing, or event that prefigures a New Testament person, thing, or event. Job, by virtue of his suffering, is a type (from the Greek word for "mold") or figure of Christ; Christ is thus the antitype of Job. (Notice that the antitype is not the opposite of the type, but is a higher development of the type.) Other types of Christ: Adam, as head of the race; Joseph, as redeemer of the brothers who sold him; Moses, as giver of bread (manna) and water. Eden is a type of the Church that the Christian enters at baptism, and of the Heaven in which the saints live after death. (Consult E. Auerbach, *Scenes from the Drama of European Literature;* and H. Gardner, *The Business of Criticism*, pp. 90–95, 142–43.)

ubi sunt. (Latin: "where are they?") A °motif especially common in medieval literature, emphasizing the transiency of life and human glory by asking where now are persons or things once beautiful or powerful. An example is D. G. Rossetti's translation of François Villon's "The Ballad of Dead Ladies."

understatement. See °figurative language.

unity. Generally means something like "coherence" or "congruence"; in a unified piece the parts work together and jointly contribute to the whole. The °meter (see °versification) in a poem, for example, is relevant to the meaning, and metrical variations are functional (perhaps they emphasize an important word, perhaps they suggest disharmony by themselves being disharmonious) rather than pointless. Unity suggests "completeness" or "pattern" resulting from a controlling intelligence. R. L. Stevenson, complaining about arbitrary unhappy endings, explained to James Barrie: "If you are going to make a book end badly, it must end badly from the beginning." A current °metaphor, **organic unity,** likens an artistic creation (poem, novel, etc.) to an organism (*i.e.*, a living thing) rather than to a mechanism. A watch consists of parts stuck together; its total is the sum of its separable parts, and it can be analyzed by being dissected. A living organism, however, allegedly consists of parts so inseparable that none can without fundamental damage be separated from the others. The idea that a work of art is like an organism rather than like a machine is common in much criticism from Coleridge on, but it goes back at least to Plato's *Phaedrus,* wherein Socrates says that a speech "ought to be put together like a living creature . . . not headless or footless." Often "organic unity" does not mean much more than "having no or few replaceable parts." (See °plot and °form. On organic unity, consult M. H. Abrams, *The Mirror and the Lamp.*) The **Three Unities,** formulated by Renaissance dramatic critics, are the unities of action, time, and place. A play should have no subplot (see °plot) or scenes irrelevant to the action, should not cover more than twenty-four hours, and should not have more than one locale. These rules were supposedly derived from Aristotle's *Poetics,* but he insists only that the action be unified; he observes that most plays cover less than a day; he does not even mention unity of place. (Consult H. B. Charlton, *Castelvetro's Theory of Poetry.*)

universal. See °concrete.

Utopia. A republic invented by Sir Thomas More, in his Latin °romance (1516). The name puns on Greek *ou topia* (no place) and *eu topia* (good place;) in short, Utopia is a nonexistent ideal community, usually remote in time or in place. **Utopian literature** creates an imaginary – sometimes admittedly impractical – government, often to °satirize real governments. Examples are Plato's *Republic* (written over a thousand years before More's work), Bacon's *The New Atlantis,* and Edward Bellamy's *Looking Back-*

ward. (Consult G. Negley and J. M. Patrick, ed., *The Quest for Utopia; Daedalus* [Spring 1965]; and R. C. Elliott, *The Shape of Utopia.*) Aldous Huxley's *Brave New World* and George Orwell's *1984* are reverse utopias, showing ideally hideous societies. (On such anti-utopias, see M. R. Hillegas, *The Future as Nightmare.*)

vehicle. See °figurative language.

vers de société. See °light verse.

vers libre. See °versification.

verse. See °versification and °literature.

versification. Paul Fussell, in *Poetic Meter and Poetic Form,* suggests that meter has three chief functions: it heightens attention, tending toward ritual; metrical variations can reinforce emotional effects, add emphasis, and imitate the meaning (*e.g.*, they can suggest lightness); traditional meters have associations, and thus this particular elegy (or limerick) in some measure can participate in the "meaning" of other poems.

The technical vocabulary of **prosody** (the study of the principles of verse structure, including meter, rhyme, sound effects, and stanzaic patterns) is large; the following are the chief terms.

In classical Greek and Latin verse the units of measurement are based on the length of time it takes to pronounce long and short syllables (**quantitative verse**). In Chinese, pitch is of paramount importance. In Japanese and in Romance languages, verse is often measured by the number of syllables in the line; but **syllabic verse** is rare in English, although Marianne Moore has written some notable poems in it, for example "The Fish," where each of the five-line stanzas is organized on a 1–3–9–6–8 syllable count. Almost all English poetry, however, is based on **stress.** The **meter** (except in Old English poetry) is the more or less regular pattern of stressed (relatively heavily **accented**) and unstressed (relatively unaccented) syllables in a line of poetry. Notice that the metrical pattern is almost never constant throughout a poem; the basic meter of a poem, however, is determined by the metrical foot that appears most regularly in the lines.

In a line of poetry the **foot** is the basic unit of measurement. It is on rare occasions a single stressed syllable; but generally a foot consists of two or three syllables, one of which is stressed. (Stress is indicated by the mark ′ ; lack of stress by ⌣ .) The repetition of feet, then, produces a pattern of stresses throughout the poem. In reading a poem, of course, not all stresses are given equal emphasis; the sense, for example, will cause some stresses to be much heavier than others. Some "stressed" syllables are almost equal to unstressed syllables and sometimes there is a **hovering stress,** that is, the stress is equally distributed over two adjacent syllables. A poet varies his metrics according to his purpose; he ought not to be so monotonously regular that he is (in W. H. Auden's words) an "accentual pest." The most common feet in English poetry are:

iamb (adjective: **iambic**): one unstressed syllable followed by one stressed syllable. The iamb, said to be the most common pattern in English speech, is surely the most common in English poetry. It is called a **rising meter,** the foot rising toward the stress. The following example has five iambic feet:

> I saw | the sky | descend | ing black | and white.
>
> (Richard Wilbur)

trochee (trochaic): one stressed syllable followed by one unstressed; a **falling meter,** the foot falling away from the stress.

> Let her | live to | earn her | dinner. (J. M. Synge)

When substituted for an iamb at the beginning of a line, a trochee can suggest weight or power, as in this line from Milton's "Lycidas":

> Shatter | your leaves.

But it can also suggest a sudden pause, as Fussell points out (*Poetic Meter and Poetic Form,* p. 65) in Keats's

> He star'd at the Pacific – and all his men
> Look'd at each other with a wild surmise –
> Silent, upon a peak in Darien.

anapest (anapestic): two unstressed syllables followed by one stressed; a rising meter.

> There are man | y who say | that a dog | has his day.
>
> (Dylan Thomas)

dactyl (dactylic): one stressed syllable followed by two unstressed; a falling meter.

> Take her up | tenderly. (Hood)

spondee (spondaic): two stressed syllables; most often used as a substitute for an iamb or trochee; it neither rises nor falls, and it commonly suggests weight or labor.

Smart lad, | to slip | betimes | away.   (A. E. Housman)

The **amphibrach** is a foot of 3 syllables, the middle being the most heavily stressed or the longest (*e.g.*, "allegiance"); in the **amphimacer,** also a foot of 3 syllables, the middle is the least stressed or shortest (*e.g.*, "parallel"). Because the **pyrrhic** foot (two unstressed syllables) lacks a stress, it is often not considered a legitimate foot in English. It commonly suggests speed or ease.

A metrical line consists of one or more feet and is named for the number of feet in it. The following names are used:

monometer: one foot (infrequent in English poetry), as in these lines on fleas:

Adam
Had 'em.

dimeter: two feet.

trimeter: three feet.

tetrameter: four feet.

pentameter: five feet.

hexameter: six feet; if in iambics, a hexameter is called an **Alexandrine,** as in the second line of the following:

A needless Alexandrine ends the song
That, like a wounded snake, drags its slow length along.   (Pope)

heptameter (or **septenary,** or, if in iambics, a **fourteener**): seven feet.

octameter: eight feet.

A line is scanned for the kind and number of feet in it, and the **scansion** tells you if it is, say, anapestic trimeter (three anapests):

As I came | to the edge | of the woods.   (Frost)

Another example, this time iambic pentameter:

The land | was ours | before | we were | the land's.   (Frost)

The omission of one or more final unstressed syllables, often a variant in trochaic measure, is **catalexis:**

Irish | poets | learn your | trade.   (Yeats)

The addition of one or more unstressed syllables at the beginning or end of a line is **hypermeter.** If the addition comes at the beginning of a line it may also be called **anacrusis.** A line ending with an additional unstressed syllable has a **feminine ending;** a line ending with a stressed syllable (not additional) has a **masculine ending.** The **caesura** (usually indicated by the symbol //) is a slight pause within the line. It need not be indicated by punctuation, and it does not affect the metrical count:

> Know then thyself,//presume not God to scan;
> The proper study of Mankind//is Man. (Pope)

An **end-stopped line** concludes with a distinct syntactical pause. Both of the following lines are end-stopped.

> True ease in writing comes from art, not chance,
> As those move easiest who have learned to dance. (Pope)

A **run-on line** has its sense carried over into the next line without syntactical pause. This running-over is also known as **enjambment.**

> At the round earth's imagined corners blow
> Your trumpets, angels. (Donne)

If the syllable ending the run-on line receives only a light metrical stress (as on such words as "and," "if," "in"), it is a **weak ending.**

In **sprung rhythm** (a term coined by Gerard Manley Hopkins) a foot has one stressed syllable, which begins the foot, and any number of unstressed syllables. Note how the following lines (in an example given by Hopkins) each have three stressed syllables, but varying numbers of unstressed ones.

> Díng, | dóng, | béll;
>
> Púss˘y's | ín ˘the | wéll;
>
> Whó | pút ˘her | ín?
>
> Lít˘tle | Jóhn˘ny | Thín.

(For a discussion of Hopkins's complicated versification consult W. J. Ong's essay in *Immortal Diamond*, ed. N. Weyand; and P. F. Baum, "Sprung Rhythm," *Publications of the Modern Language Association*, 74 [1959], 418–25.)

Meter produces **rhythm,** recurrences at equal intervals, but rhythm (from a Greek word meaning "flow") is usually applied to larger units than feet. Often it depends most obviously on pauses. Thus, a poem with run-on lines will have a different rhythm from a poem with end-stopped lines, even though both are in the same meter. And prose, though it is unmetrical, can thus have rhythm too. In addition to being affected by syntactical pauses, rhythm is affected by pauses due to consonant clusters and the length of words. Polysyllabic words establish a different rhythm from monosyllabic words, even in metrically identical lines. One can say, then, that rhythm is altered by shifts in meter, syntax, and the length and ease of pronunciation. But even with no such shift, even if a line is repeated verbatim, a reader may sense a change in rhythm. The rhythm of the final line of a poem may well differ from that of the line before, even though in all other respects the lines are identical, as in Frost's "Stopping by Woods," which concludes by repeating "And miles to go before I sleep." One may simply sense that this final line ought to be spoken, say, more slowly.

Though rhythm is basic to poetry, **rhyme** is not. Rhyme is the repetition of the identical or similar stressed sound or sounds. It is, presumably, pleasant in itself; it suggests order; and it also may be related to meaning, for it brings two words sharply together, often implying a relationship, as, for example, Pope's "throne" and "alone." (Consult W. K. Wimsatt, Jr., "One Relation of Rhyme to Reason," in his *The Verbal Icon.*) **Perfect** or **exact rhymes** occur when differing consonant-sounds are followed by identical stressed vowel-sounds, and the following sounds, if any, are identical (foe : toe; meet : fleet; buffer : rougher). Notice that perfect rhyme involves identity of sound, not of spelling. "Fix" and "sticks," like "buffer" and "rougher," are perfect rhymes.

In **half-rhyme** (or **slant-rhyme, approximate-rhyme, near-rhyme, off-rhyme**) only the final consonant-sounds of the rhyming words are identical; the stressed vowel-sounds as well as the initial consonant-sounds, if any, differ (soul : oil; firth : forth; trolley : bully). **Eye-rhyme** is not really rhyme; it merely looks like rhyme (cough : bough : rough). The final syllables in **masculine rhyme** are stressed and, after their differing initial consonant-sounds, are identical in sound (stark : mark; support : retort). In **feminine rhyme** (or **double-rhyme**) stressed rhyming syllables are followed by identical unstressed syllables (revival : arrival; flatter : batter). **Triple-rhyme** is a kind of feminine rhyme in which identical stressed vowel-sounds are followed by two identical unstressed syllables (machinery : scenery; tenderly : slenderly). **End-rhyme** (or **terminal-rhyme**) has the rhyming word at the end of the line. **Internal-rhyme** has at least one of the rhyming words within the line (Wilde's "Each narrow *cell* in which we *dwell*"). **Alliteration** (or **initial-rhyme**) is a repetition of initial sounds in two or more words: "*B*ring me my *b*ow of *b*urning gold"; "*All* the *aw*ful *au*guries." In Macbeth's phrase: "after life's fitful fever," true alliteration is found in the repeated *f*'s of *f*itful *f*ever, and **medial alliteration** in the *f*'s of a*f*ter, li*f*e's, and fit*f*ul, which are not in initial positions. In **Assonance** identical vowel-sounds are preceded and followed by differing consonant-sounds, in words in proximity. "Tide" and "hide" are rhymes; "tide," "mine" are assonantal. **Consonance** is identical consonant-sounds and differing vowel-sounds in words in proximity (fail : feel; rough : roof; pitter : patter). Sometimes consonance is more loosely defined merely as the repetition of a consonant (fai*l* : pee*l*). **Onomatopoeia** (Greek for "the making of words") is the invention or use of a word whose sound echoes or suggests its meaning. "Hiss" and "buzz" are onomatopoetic. There is a mistaken tendency to see onomatopoeia everywhere, for example in "thunder" and "horror." Many words sometimes thought to be onomatopoetic are not clearly imitative of the thing they denote; they merely contain some sounds which – when we know what the word means – seem to have some resemblance to the thing they denote. (Consult R. A. Brower, *The Fields of Light*, pp. 71–74.)

Just as prose is organized into paragraphs, so lines of poetry that have unity form a **verse paragraph.** Often (but not always) the unity is aided by rhymes, and the paragraph thus may coincide with a stanza. A **stanza** (Italian: literally, "a stopping place") is a unit consisting of group of lines; it usually has a fixed rhyme-pattern repeated throughout the poem. A stanza thus is a large rhythmical unit containing smaller rhythmical units, lines. A stanza is sometimes called a **verse,** though "verse" may also mean a single line of poetry. (In discussing stanzas, rhymes are indicated by identical letters. Thus, *aabba* indicates that the first, second, and fifth lines rhyme with each other, while the third and fourth lines are linked by a different rhyme. An unrhymed line is denoted by *x*.) Common stanzaic forms in English poetry are the following:

couplet: stanza of two lines, usually, but not necessarily, with end-rhymes. "Couplet" is also used for a pair of rhyming lines. The **octosyllabic couplet** is iambic or trochaic tetrameter:

> Had we but world enough, and time,
> This coyness, lady, were no crime. (Marvell)

heroic couplet: a rhyming couplet of iambic pentameter, often "closed," *i.e.*, containing a complete thought, with a fairly heavy pause at the end of the first line and a still heavier one at the end of the second. Commonly there is a parallel or an antithesis within a line, or between the two lines. It is called heroic because in England, especially in the eighteenth century, it was much used for heroic (°epic) poems.

> Some foreign writers, some our own despise;
> The ancients only, or the moderns, prize. (Pope)

triplet (or **tercet**): a three-line stanza, usually with one rhyme.

> Whenas in silks my Julia goes
> Then, then (methinks) how sweetly flows
> That liquefaction of her clothes. (Herrick)

terza rima: a three-line stanza linked by rhyme to the next stanza: *aba bcb cdc*, etc. Shelley's "Ode to the West Wind" is an example.

quatrain: a four-line stanza, rhymed or unrhymed. The **heroic** (or **elegiac**) **quatrain** is iambic pentameter, rhyming *abab*. The **ballad stanza** is a quatrain alternating iambic tetrameter with iambic trimeter lines, usually rhyming *xbxb*. Sometimes it is followed by a **refrain,** a line or lines repeated several times (see °ballad).

rhyme royal: a seven-line stanza of iambic pentameter, rhyming *ababbcc*. (It is called "royal" because James I of Scotland used it, but he had been anticipated in England by Chaucer.)

ottava rima: an eight-line stanza of iambic pentameter, rhyming *abababcc*. **Spenserian stanza:** a nine-line stanza, rhyming *ababbcbcc*, named for its originator, Edmund Spenser (1552?–99). The first eight lines are iambic pentameter, the last line is an Alexandrine (*i.e.*, hexameter, see above).

sonnet: for the Elizabethans, sonnet and °lyric were often synonymous, but sonnet has come to mean a poem of fourteen lines (occasionally twelve or sixteen). The meter, if in English, is iambic pentameter; the rhyme is usually according to one of the following schemes. The **Italian** (or **Petrarchan**) **sonnet** has two divisions: the first eight lines are the **octave,** the last six are the **sestet,** rhyming *abba abba cde cde;* the sestet sometimes is *cd cd cd,* or a variant. Milton, Wordsworth, and Keats have written notable sonnets in the Italian form. The **English** (or **Shakespearean**) **sonnet** is usually arranged into three quatrains and a couplet, rhyming *abab cdcd efef gg*. In many sonnets there is a marked correspondence between the rhyme scheme and the development of the thought. Thus an Italian sonnet may state a generalization in the octave, and a specific example in the sestet. Or an English sonnet may give three examples – one in each quatrain – and draw a conclusion in the couplet. (For example, see p. 56.) A

sonnet sequence (such as those by Petrarch, Shakespeare, and Sidney) is a group of sonnets which form not so much a connected narrative as a related series of lyrical explorations, usually on love, love betrayed, love renewed, etc. Some notable sonnet sequences since Shakespeare are Elizabeth Barrett Browning's *Sonnets from the Portuguese*, George Meredith's *Modern Love*, W. H. Auden's *The Quest*, and Dylan Thomas's *Altarwise by Owl-light*. (Consult J. W. Lever, *The Elizabethan Love Sonnet*.)

blank verse: unrhymed iambic pentameter. Introduced into English poetry by Surrey in the middle of the sixteenth century, late in the century it became the standard medium (especially in the hands of Marlowe and Shakespeare) of English °drama. In the seventeenth century, Milton used it for his °epic, *Paradise Lost*, and it has continued to be used in both dramatic and nondramatic literature. Example:

> Time hath, my Lord, a wallet at his back,
> Wherein he puts alms for oblivion. (Shakespeare)

doggerel: rhyming lines which are comic by virtue of their irregular metrics and metrics made regular at the cost of stressing normally unstressed syllables.

> More peevish, cross, and splenetic
> Than dog distract or monkey sick. (Butler)

If the subject-matter is mock-heroic (see °burlesque) and the lines are iambic tetrameter couplets (as in the example just quoted), the poem is often called **Hudibrastic,** after Samuel Butler's *Hudibras*.

free verse (or ***vers libre***): rhythmical lines varying in length, adhering to no fixed metrical pattern, and usually unrhymed. The pattern is often largely based on repetition and parallel grammatical structure. Though such a form may appear unrestrained, as T. S. Eliot (a practitioner) said, "No *vers* is *libre* for the man who wants to do a good job." Robert Frost, however, didn't see the point of it: he said he "would as soon write free verse as play tennis with the net down." The following example is from Whitman's "Song of Myself":

> I celebrate myself, and sing myself,
> And what I assume you shall assume,
> For every atom belonging to me as good belongs to you.

(Consult P. F. Baum, *The Principles of English Versification;* and P. Fussell, *Poetic Meter and Poetic Form*.)

Victorian. Of or pertaining to the reign of Queen Victoria (reigned 1837–1901) of England. A period characterized by industrial expansion, scientific discovery, and religious conflict. More narrowly, this term is used (inaccurately) to characterize the period as narrow-minded, smug, prudish, moralistic. (Consult W. E. Houghton, *The Victorian Frame of Mind;* G. M. Young, *Portrait of an Age;* and *From Dickens to Hardy,* ed. B. Ford.)

voice. See °persona.

weak ending. See °versification.

well-made play. See °*pièce bien faite.*

wipe. See °cuts.

wit. For a brief history of the term, and its relevance to laughter, see °comedy. See also °irony.

zeugma. Strictly speaking it denotes the use of a verb which governs two or more nouns though the verb is literally suited only to one. An example is: "Warmed by fire and laughter." But the definition has been widened, and the verb need not be used figuratively so long as its meaning changes somewhat, *e.g.,* Queen Anne "does sometimes council take – and sometimes tea."

zoom freeze and **zoom shot.** See °shot.